And One More Thing

Quentin Crisp

BOOKS

Edited by Phillip Ward
and
Laurence Watts

Front cover photograph by Joseph Mulligan

ISBN: 0692168095
ISBN-13: 978-0692168097

CONTENTS

FOREWORD

YOU MAY BE FORGIVEN FOR thinking that 2017's *The Last Word* – the third and final installment in Quentin Crisp's autobiography – was his last book. After all, in it he states that, "This will be the last book that I shall write. My swan song, if you will. A chance for me to have the last word." Quentin was, of course, absolutely right. *The Last Word* was his last book. And yet so is this.

When my co-editor, Phillip Ward, and I sat down to edit the manuscript that he and Quentin had produced after many hours of interviews and dictation, we reasoned that it was best split into two works. *The Last Word* was to be the first – in which Quentin summed up his life, his approaching death, and his philosophy – and the second is this, *And One More Thing*, in which Quentin primarily shares his views on other people, their lives and their views.

And One More Thing is not a book of continuous prose. It is not meant to be. Instead, it contains the final musings and thoughts of Quentin that we could not fit into *The Last Word*. We present them here as vignettes, alongside his collected poetry, his apology, the transcript of his 'Alternative Christmas Message', and the script of his one-man show.

The material for this book was dictated by Quentin to Phillip Ward in sessions that took place in the two years before his passing (1998-1999). In his advanced age, Quentin would frequently veer off subject. Such material didn't fit into the narrative of *The Last Word*, so we include it here, fearful that leaving it unpublished would be doing a disservice to Quentin's legacy.

In the 'vignettes' section you will find Quentin talking about all manner of people from flapper girls to Monica Lewinsky, and from the British Royal Family to Walt Disney. Some subject matter will be familiar to fans of Quentin while others will be new.

Next, we include the texts of his infamous apology to the gay community and his Alternative Christmas Message. The original Christmas Message, sometimes inaccurately called the Queen's Speech, is an annual address by the British monarch to her subjects, broadcast on Christmas Day on the BBC. Quentin was the first person chosen to make an unofficial address, also broadcast on Christmas Day, on Channel 4, which began in 1993 with Quentin and continues to this day.

Then we present the collected poetry of Quentin Crisp. He wrote a good many poems. Those included here have been collected by Phillip Ward from a variety of sources. Quentin always meant to include his poetry in his final literary work, and a good deal of effort was made by him in trying to recall his poems in the last years of his life.

Lastly, we include the transcript from the scripted element of Quentin's one-man show *An Evening With Quentin Crisp*. This transcript was made by Phillip Ward, based on Quentin's performance of the show in New York City in 1999, and was edited and rewritten by Quentin. It is therefore the version he would have performed in England later that year. Of course, Quentin was never able to perform it on tour in England that year, passing as he did on November 21, 1999, not long after touching down in Great Britain. Quentin was ninety years old.

There is beauty in *And One More Thing* as well as a sense of completeness. If there are errors, please consider these ours and not Quentin's. Our motivation in compiling this book has been to ensure that fans of Quentin have access to as much of his previously unpublished work as possible.

Laurence Watts & Phillip Ward
December 2018

VIGNETTES

1. SUPERMODELS, FASHION AND BEAUTY

Previously I have stated that, had I been born a woman, I would not have wanted to have been particularly beautiful or striking. That would have attracted too much of the wrong kind of attention, which would have in turn necessitated, or at least demanded, more of me physically than I have ever been willing to give another person.

I am not certain however that, had I been female, my sense of fashion would be any different from what it is now.

People have, at different times, described my look as flashy. It is no such thing. It is merely the product of what clothing has been gifted to me over the years. I never shop for clothes. I am not fashionable. The pronouncements I have made on style come not from an adherence to fashion, but from a practical disconnection from it that enables me to observe others.

That being said, I confess I have never understood women's desire to be fashionable. It is such a waste of time, which is why I personally eschew it. But they run towards it. They want it urgently. Fiercely. If short skirts are 'in', they rush home and shorten their skirts or they buy them in overpriced stores.

A woman once told me of her dilemma. She said: "You think you're impervious to fashion. When the fashion for short skirts arrives, you think, 'I shan't do anything about it. I shall wear long skirts.' But within about two days, you can feel your skirt flapping about your ankles. And in some way, you are affected to want to be fashionable."

Thus, women are 'victims' of fashion. But why are men not victims of fashion? I suppose certain men are. Actors for example. But they are not affected to the same extent that women are. Women are mortified when they are caught wearing something that is not fashionable.

Make no mistake however, fashion is not equal to style. It exists instead of it. When you don't know who you are, you consult the glossy magazines. Then, all we know when we see you coming down the street is that you had enough money to buy *Vanity Fair*. That's not what style is. Style is not stylishness. The latter of the two words has been corrupted nowadays to mean something else.

If you base your style on glossy magazines you can, of course, adapt the current style to yourself. You can make use of it and remain the same. But there can be all sorts of problems. Can you wear very short skirts if you have terrible legs? That's something you really have to make up your own mind about. Women, after all, want to be attractive regardless of the current fad.

When short skirts above the knee came in, I was horrified to see them sported by women with legs like horses. They looked horrifying, but nevertheless they still wore short skirts and presumably considered themselves to be fashionable. It's a three-way war: how to be attractive, how to be yourself, and how to be fashionable. It's a very difficult equation.

And it's arbitrary because the fashion industry is, of course, really governed by the manufacturers rather than designers. There is an industry surplus of wool and so wool becomes fashionable. Some new type or color of fabric is invented and so that becomes fashionable. All of a sudden shops are flooded with brown - light brown, dark brown, and so on. But why wear it if brown isn't a color that emphasizes your best features and detracts from your faults?

These days supermodels have overtaken superstars in popularity. I think this is because they are nearer to us. Superstars live 'over there' in Hollywood, which is at a distance from most Americans. Otherwise they are only depicted on the silver screen, through which one cannot hope to get their attention. By contrast, supermodels are walking up and down catwalks only a few feet away from us. They appear more accessible. Superstars could only do the equivalent with hordes of security guards to assist them.

And supermodels are so thin. Impossibly thin. So thin that clothes can be put on them in just a matter of seconds. Because without anyone thinking about it, they go off stage, smiling, someone takes hold of them, rips their clothes off and puts new clothes on them. Then they go back on the catwalk again. But because they are so thin nothing ever gets torn.

I've never seen anything work on the catwalk that someone could wear in real life. I once saw a model walking down the catwalk with her hands on her breasts to prevent them jumping out from her dress. Then there was another woman with a backless bead costume down to the end of her spine. If she had turned a quick turn, the whole thing would have fallen off. At another show there were women with fringes on the front of their shoes. In any real-world setting they would be forever saying, "You're standing on my fringe! Thank you." Of course, they all looked beautiful, but everything was always so impractical.

My suspicion is that, once the fashion show is over, the designers collect up all the fabric that's been displayed, take it back into the workroom and remake it into real clothes for everyday people.

I remember once meeting Vivienne Westwood, who was quite extraordinary. I didn't know who she was initially, but after we were introduced it became apparent that I knew her in a time gone by. We met during New York Fashion Week. Her collection was good, but the show was not. It was a bit untidy, a bit awkward. There was a great mock stone entrance for the girls to enter by, which unfortunately meant that they had to stoop down in order to enter. And that sort of spoiled everything. You can't really creep onto the catwalk. What kind of an entrance is that? But the clothes were good. And the clothes were more realistic than they are at most shows.

Ms. Westwood's clothes were made of wool. Alas, the models had horrible hair, which detracted from rather than enhanced the look of the clothes. I don't know why they did that. They all looked like they had just got out of bed. And there were various mistakes in the show as well that were obvious to onlookers. Those are the worst kind of mistakes. There was no passing them off as deliberate actions.

I am told Ms. Westwood is very, very rich. So, I suppose all the effort that goes into these shows, her collections and her public persona is worth it. But I don't think I would wear any of her fashion. Principally, of course, that is because all of her designs are for women, but there is also an aesthetic judgement I am making. Yes, her clothes were more acceptable as street clothes than a lot of the other shows I have seen, but they nevertheless weren't my kind of style. I'm sure she's not worried. I don't think I am the kind of person she is designing for anyway. I shouldn't be as I never buy anything.

I can see why she's successful though. If fashion shows are meant for buyers, then I could see how a buyer would look at her collection and say "I could sell that in my shops." Too often it seems as though fashion shows are meant for something else entirely. They seem to be more of a way to get your name known to everybody, with outlandish photos in the newspapers and stunts meant purely for shock value. And if this truly is their purpose they are a poor form of live entertainment.

Ms. Westwood has a husband. He is a young man and when I met him he was wearing a black kilt. He seemed very nice. He was there at the show and he was at the party afterwards. He didn't say anything, not to me or anyone else. But at both the fashion show and the afterparty, even though both were such great to-dos, no one ever said very much. I'm guessing he was about thirty years old. She's about fifty. A very spritely fifty though, and with hair the color of breakfast food. And she's very unassuming. In spite of all her fame and wealth, she wasn't flinging herself about but behaving in a very circumspect way.

Another time I saw a Todd Oldham show, which, though very efficient and very beautiful, was totally impractical. Absolutely nothing worn on the catwalk that night could be worn by real people. I said to my companion, who sat next to me for the show, "Could any of these girls get into a taxi wearing any of these clothes?" He didn't think so. It was all too much. Too over the top.

But Mr. Oldham's show was very efficient. There were always two girls on the catwalk, one coming and one going, and always walking very fast. They had to walk quickly because they had to fit the show into just three-quarters of an hour. So, the models strode forward, they twitched in front of the cameras, and then they scuttled quickly backstage. It was almost Germanic in its execution.

The fashion industry proves that beauty is most definitely not in the eye of the beholder. Beauty is in the eye of the possessor. A woman who feels beautiful can convince other people that is what she is. The fashion industry revolves around this point. And I think it's a point that applies particularly to women. Men aren't supposed to care whether they're beautiful or not. I think they do, but they're supposed not to. But women are allowed by society to bask in their beauty. And if they feel they are beautiful, they have a relaxed sort of glow which spreads all around them.

Of course, people say that beauty is in the eye of the beholder because some will find beauty in others whom no one else thinks is beautiful. But such situations ignore the general consensus of what makes someone beautiful. It's easy to create a list of these attributes, but these are essentially the commonalities you see between models and television and film stars. I don't know how we've come to have a universal view of what is beautiful but, by whatever process it is, it's also true that every age has had a different view of what beauty is.

The previous age to ours admired women with sloping shoulders and rather large arms, so that you couldn't see the elbow or the wrist. Consequently, all the women wore dresses that best displayed these qualities, if they had them. And they had smooth necks, small hands, small feet, small waists and wide hips. These days, of course, in order to be considered beautiful you're meant to be stick thin, straight up and down.

From time to time, I'm asked if I have any beauty tips. I do not. My only advice is rather general, which is that you should keep on applying make-up until you look the way you want to be. Then you should stop. The mistake that people make is to pile on more and more make-up as you get older. This is a great mistake. You don't end up looking younger from this kind of heavy application, you end up looking like other old people who are trying equally as hard to look young, which is to say you look old. You actually need less as time goes by, not more.

I've also been asked my opinion on tattoos, which to me is a form of bodily disfigurement rather than enhancement. I have never been able to fathom why anyone would wish to have his or her body permanently spoiled and scarred by a tattoo artist, but it is a practice that is increasing in popularity here in America, and one that a great number of women have now also decided to undertake.

When I had any pride in my body, I wanted it to be totally my own. Not disfigured by strange mottos or rudimentary sketches of fish or birds. Of course, now that I am old, 'the great tattoo artist' has marked my skin in all sorts of unpleasant ways. I think my own reluctance to get a tattoo, when perhaps I was closer to the right age for one, was that such an action was too manly a practice to suit my idea of myself.

Tattooing was originally done by sailors who wished, for some unknown reason, to be identified should they wash up on a foreign shore. But now that nobody washes up on a foreign shore, I think tattooing has just become a sort of a peer-group test. Most tribes have tests for would-be warriors, and I think getting a tattoo has become a modern-day equivalent. It's a test of endurance, because the application of a tattoo is painful. The less you flinch at the pain the more manly you are considered I would imagine, or something like that anyway.

You see, in primitive life when the tribe was perpetually threatened either by nature or by some other tribe, everybody had to be strong. Everyone had to be ready to take up their arms, or whatever it was that they fought with, and fight. They didn't want anyone who was going to turn and run away. So, that's why they had these rites of passage. Nowadays the motivation of peer pressure within groups of friends, which are our modern equivalent of tribes, is less obvious. It seems more like herd mentality to me.

I had never met a tattoo artist until I was introduced by a German film director to Mr. Spider Webb[1]. When I told him that I thought he was weird, he said to me,

"If I seem weird to you, then I'm really worried."

But now that I know that he is a real artist, I've revised my opinion of him. I think that he uses the backs of his friends as a sort of sketchpad, where he works out the designs of his real pictures. His tattoos are mainly abstract but resemble certain forms of plant life. This I know because his victims are forever stripping proudly in public to display his handiwork.

I don't know how far Mr. Spider Webb goes, but I have read a fascinating book by a writer called Mr. Samuel Steward, who, under the nom de plume Phil Sparrow, earned his living as a tattooist. In this capacity he is said to have tattooed the penis of a policeman, during which process the officer - off-duty one assumes - ejaculated.

One can only assume, given the outcome, that pain had become his true pleasure and he was a bona fide masochist. Nevertheless, it's a little difficult to understand what purpose such a tattoo would serve, since the picture or message could only be fully seen or read when the gentleman's penis was in 'full bloom'. Not exactly the time

---

[1] Real name: Mr. Joseph O'Sullivan.

you would want to enter an art gallery and be seen. Well, not for most people, anyway. The policeman may have thought differently.

2. CHILDREN

Children are an awful thing. Living in America, one cannot help but notice how much American men like their children however. It's altogether different to how children are perceived and treated in England.

Here, men talk to their children, play with their children and carry their children. They even kiss them, which is unheard of in England. My father never dreamt of kissing anybody, let alone me. And he would never have carried any of us. If ever we went somewhere, he always walked ahead of my mother by a good few yards. We all followed along behind. It was as if he was detached from the whole process of family life. But in America there is a strange bond between the son and the father, especially if there is only one son within the brood.

In England, married women never have a minute to spare. You call on certain people at their house and they come to the door holding one child by the hand and with another child held to their bosom. And when you are with them, they call out into other rooms: "What are you doing in there? Margery, you sound very quiet." They worry endlessly about all of their children and what they are doing. If they are not in the room with them, why are they not in the room? If they are in the room with them, will they keep quiet?

I would hate to live like that, but most women do and have chosen to do it. They got married so that someone would pay their rent. I think that is genuinely the only reason why working-class women get married. Then they have about four children and have to look after them all of their lives. When the youngest is seven or eight, they can be left alone in the house for only a moment, because even then they may set the house on fire.

I don't know why, but there are endless reports on television of a woman who has been arrested because she left her children alone. She had to do it! She can't go out to the shops with all her children, because they run about and take things off the shelves, and then she's accused of stealing. She can't control a whole gang of children, so in these instances she decides to leave them at home. And then, of course, they throw themselves out of the window, or they set fire to the place. No one knows why. But there is no way to win, so the moral here is don't have children.

Clearly, I have never had children. I have neither married nor ever had sex with a woman. So, I was never likely to have children. And at least partially because of this, I have never contemplated a life with children. But I know I would have hated it. Ultimately, had I fathered children I believe I would have behaved badly and I would have hit them. I don't think there would have been an alternative. You just can't talk to children and, of course, talking is my favorite pastime. It's the only thing that I'm good at.

If I had been a woman, I would have tried not to have children. I don't know whether as a woman you can have an operation the same way you can when you're a man. I believe you can only have a hysterectomy, which I would have hesitated to do. Here in America a doctor might even refuse to perform the operation on religious or moral grounds. I once heard about a doctor who refused to give a man a vasectomy. The doctor refused saying, "I won't do it. Why should I let him indulge himself?" His issue seemed to be that afterwards, sex would go from being chiefly about procreation to solely about titillation. It was a kind of puritanism that the doctor was following. But it makes no sense. Even for married couples, sex is only about procreation once, twice or maybe three times in a lifetime. It's far too expensive a pastime to maintain after that.

Gay men have, of course, mastered the art of sex for titillation's sake. They have so many oats to sow it's surprising they have time for anything else. Lesbians are different. So, even if the whole world became gay, there would still be children being born because of all the turkey-baster babies that lesbians have.

I don't understand why lesbians want children. The trap must look so enticing to them though. Initially, you get to dress your children in pretty clothes. Then they learn to say Mama and Dada and parents coo and crow. But then they grow up to be taller than you and they start to have ideas about the world and themselves with which you disagree. And at that point all you can say is, "It didn't say any of this on the box. Why can't I get my money back? Why can't I throw them away?"

I think, at the appropriate age, and in the right set of circumstances, parents should be able to legally sacrifice their children and be done with the whole thing.

If you insist on raising children all the way to adulthood, I think the most important thing is to raise a child to be free. Children should be nurtured to have their own opinions. Not to come to you the whole time asking, "What shall I do? What should I say." No. When you ask them, "What would you like to do?" They should be able to tell you. If they say, "I don't know," then they're in trouble.

Build them into decisive people, for their own good. Try not to suffocate them with art, literature or music. That is a mistake because life is there and they have to trudge through it. And if you can prevent them from bullying other people, or being bullied by other people, that too would be a good thing.

A woman I knew once said, "It is as much of a sin to allow yourself to be exploited as it is to exploit others", and that I hadn't thought of. But it's no good saying to children, "Well stand up for yourself", because what if you can't stand up for yourself? I couldn't stand up for myself and I didn't, and the wider world knew I couldn't, but I survived by simply appealing for help and understanding.

That's something that worries me about people. Some people have no capacity to appeal to others for help. They want to be independent and they bolster this view by saying, "You had better learn how to do it because no one's going to show you." But people will show you how to do it, and in return you've only got to be grateful for their help. It worries me that the philosophy of the helpless is something that has to be gone into. To me, it is self-evident, though of course I have been helpless my whole life.

The pursuit of parenthood is something I've never understood and yet it is near-universal. My father lived in debt and, though I didn't know that at the time, I think I may have been influenced by it. He didn't want to give anything away. He must have been a very bad lawyer, because lawyers mostly succeed. He'd been a lawyer all his life, but when he died he had given my mother four children and nothing more. He left her no money. It was a terrible thing. I disliked him for various reasons, chiefly because he disliked me, but I realize now that he was a contemptible character.

When my parents lived in Carshalton, before I and the brother next to me were born, they had a son and a daughter and no money. What the hell did they think they were doing having two more children? And, as I have said before, I think I was a mistake; and I think my brother, who was only fifteen months older than me, was also a mistake. How could you make the same mistake twice? My parents were sophisticated people, so they must have known about contraception. I never questioned it while either of them were alive - I wouldn't have dared - but they must have known what they were doing and I can't understand it.

Women seem to go mad if they can't have children. And I can't think why because it's so uncomfortable bearing and then giving birth to a child. I knew a woman once who said she had never had children, and then one day she did have one. I said, "What was it like?" And she said, "Oh, Quentin. The humiliation!" That was as I imagined. You lie there with your legs apart and you grunt and you groan, and everyone stands around. It must be humiliating beyond anything. But most women don't seem to mind and I can't understand it. And then when you've done it, you've got a child and you're enchained forever. A woman can never leave the house. She can't go to the movies for seventeen years!

A pet would be far less expensive, but people don't have children as pets. They have children as representatives. When you say to a woman, "How nice your children are." She says, "Thank you," as though they were an attribute to her. As though you had just praised her. And so many parents regard children as part of themselves. That is where the trouble begins because, of course, in the end most children hate their parents, which must be the worst feeling in the world. The ultimate betrayal.

These days, infertility is a huge concern for many would-be parents. And people are so desperate to have children that they will go through almost any ordeal in order to have them. They go to doctors, who tell them they must lie in a certain position when conceiving, they must take this, eat that, and not do this and not do that. And even if they follow all of these convoluted instructions, there's still no guarantee that the woman will get pregnant.

I feel like women bear most of the burden when it comes to fertility treatment. Men do not like going to doctors and finding out whether they are sterile or not. Women don't mind as much. For heterosexual men, the ability to father offspring seems to be inextricably intertwined with their own sense of masculinity. Yet very few women are sterile, so it is quite often the husband's fault that they cannot conceive.

Soon, however, physical conception may be a thing of the past if the scientists behind cloning get their way. I can't see the point myself, but that's because I believe we have more than enough children as it is. We don't want more of the same. And I can't see the point of cloning myself or anyone else for that matter. The whole point of developing a personal style is to be the only one. I don't need or want copycats.

If they offered me enough money though, I would do it. If you offered me enough money, I would do practically anything because money is the only thing I've ever really loved. It's my principal weakness. Money never lets you down the way an estranged friend can. You don't have to pander to money in order to win its favor. And money is for hoarding. Even as a child, I tried to save the money given to me. People would say, just after they had given me some money for my birthday or for Christmas, "What are you going to spend it on?" And I would reply, "Nothing. I'll just keep it."

But I digress. Returning to procreation, it's important to note that we have already passed the population explosion that Aldous Huxley[2] thought would be the end of us. So, for the fate of humanity and its future, I think something has to be done so that we don't continue to increase at an alarming rate. Because the more people there are, the more food we need to produce. We are still coping for now, but I'm sure the current situation will come violently to an end. Overpopulation will soon mean people living with their feet permanently in the sea, because we shan't have the land for them to sit on or stand on.

I presume then, we shall learn not to have children. Either because we abort them or because we sensibly decide not to have them. Currently, children are of such abundance that grandmothers have to look after their grandchildren, which is very bad for them because they have already done the parenting thing and they should be free of it. But this is because modern-day mothers are simply overwhelmed. Yet it is very bad for a child to be looked after by someone who is at the end of her tether because she is seventy and children are running amok around her house.

More sterility, that's what we need. I think men will have to be made barren in some way, voluntarily presumably because otherwise there would be a revolution.

In China, you are forbidden to have more than one child. So, of course, they are always murdering their girls because they don't want them. They are no good. They don't earn a living. But it would be better if we had fewer

---

[2] Aldous Leonard Huxley, English writer, novelist and philosopher

murders and more prevention of unwanted children being born in the first place.

As such, I do think we have to get over this ridiculous objection to abortion that some people have. An aborted child is none the wiser. No one alive has memories from the womb. It's a mercy killing in the truest sense of the word. Why would you want to bring a child into a world heading towards oblivion?

My personal objection towards children comes from the way they cramp their mother's or father's (or my) style. My second objection is that children turn into teenagers. Then you're really in trouble. Teenagers have always had the same problem: how to conform and rebel at the same time. They've solved that of course by conforming with one another and rebelling against their parents.

Teenagers think their parents are confining them in order to annoy them, and to some extent they are. But to an extent their parents' concern is genuine. They worry that their teenage child will stay out and get drunk and, not knowing what they're doing, become pregnant or get someone pregnant. Or they will get into a car when drunk, or with someone drunk, and a disaster may take place.

Parents only want to save your life so that you will grow up into a human being. They recognize the danger because they've lived long enough to see it happen either to themselves or others. Teenagers and children don't recognize this and aren't capable of understanding the potential consequences of their actions. Children think they are invincible. Parents know that they are not.

Some children are lucky and are born with genuinely doting parents. That means they really love you. It's unconditional, which is both a blessing and a curse. It's a blessing in the sense that they truly love you, but a curse because you're never going to get anyone to dote on you again like your parents do. Future relationships in such lives will never quite measure up.

Good parents want their children to be happy but, of course, they measure happiness in terms of their own values and aspirations. And there is frequently a miscommunication between children and their parents because parents seldom speak. Parents want children to just sit there, to be around, and that is very tiresome for young people. So, if I could design a perfect system, I would create one in which we didn't have parents. Everyone would be happier that way since they would have no one to disappoint.

3. SHOPPERS

The real difference between the sexes is that men shop and women go shopping. Women don't love money with the pure spiritual flame that men do. They want to convert it into objects, jewelry, furs, clothing and accessories. Men love money for its own sake. They finger checkbooks, credit cards and bank boxes as though they were fetishes. Men's prayers are not based in words but in numerals.

Until recently, money had a bad name in England. A British stage actress was once asked if the 1890s were really as naughty as they are now perceived to have been. She replied, "A peculiar morality prevailed at this time. We were once called into the office of Mr. Edwardes[3] and told that the reputation of his theatre rested on our slender shoulders. We were allowed to accept presents of flowers and candy, jewelry and furs, yachts, houses and islands, but never money."

I remember, when I was young, my sister sweeping into the room where my mother and I were sitting and stating that, "The people next door have no money to speak of."

[3] George Joseph Edwardes, one-time manager of the Gaiety Theatre, London

Doubtless she was repeating something she had heard my mother say. Nevertheless, my mother replied, "But money is never to speak of." This may have been out of self-defense however, because we didn't have any either.

When people visit my room here in New York, on Third Street, they look around aghast and say, "Do you have to live here?"

I used to say, "Yes." But that's not the whole answer.

If I knew that I would die in the next two years, I could live anywhere, but I don't. To my dismay, I seem indestructible and so must conserve my wealth. This is why I continue to live on Third Street in as humble surroundings as I do.

Why do I not advise everyone to live as I do, to renounce shopping, to buy nothing? For one thing, I don't think they would do it. But for another, all sorts of unpleasant phrases would be flung at me, particularly by shopkeepers and economists. They would accuse me of fostering a sluggish economy.

I am no economist. I don't know why money only keeps its value by being spread around, but apparently it does. Another reason why I would never advocate others stopping shopping is that I am frequently the recipient of other people's cast-offs and hand-me-downs. It would be against my own interest to advise them not to go out and shop at all.

I want to understand the retail trade. I feel vaguely that I should spend my money, but it is very difficult. The lifetime habit of thrift that I have is so hard to break. In order to spend more freely I think I would have to work. And I don't like work. It ages you terribly. So, before I do anything, before I even lift a finger, I have formed the habit of asking myself, "Could I possibly get out of this?" And if I possibly can, I do.

When I saw the excellent documentary film called *Paris is Burning*, about the poor people of Harlem, I was surprised to discover that when they were questioned by Ms. Livingston[4], who made the film, as to what they wanted in life, it transpired they wanted luxury more than that they wanted happiness.

One of her interviewees, a woman, said, "I want a swimming pool and a big car and a nice house." To me all those things would be a burden. I would have to look after each of them. Even the damned pool I would have to have cleaned every so often.

They say that the longing for luxury is the result of all the television advertisements we are bombarded with nowadays. I can't say I have noticed. When the adverts come on my television screen, I typically move about the room busying myself or making my evening meal, which consists chiefly of lumpy tea and green toast. I have never seen anything advertised on television that I would want.

I have sometimes caught advertisements announcing grand sales events, however, where everything is offered to the public at 20% off. I can't see how people know that is the case. I'm sure they just inflate their prices for the rest of the year so that they can bring them down occasionally to generate stampedes of shoppers. I wouldn't know though. I have never attended a sale in my life. Sales mean crowds and crowds of people must be avoided at all costs.

[4] Jennie Livingston, American director.

4. FRIENDS

A friend is somebody who sees your problems from your point of view. It's no good saying to someone who comes to you with his problems, "The thing is to pull yourself together," because obviously the one thing he can't do is deal with it alone. He's come to you. So, you have to absorb his personality and see the situation - which seems to you ridiculous - from his point of view, which seems serious. And then you can really be a friend. Otherwise, you're only a sort of monitor.

If someone called me their friend, that would be nice. I would have to think about whether or not I deserved the title. Whether I had really seen his or her problems from their point of view. And if I hadn't, I suppose I would have to correct my attitude until I did.

I don't have a best friend because that's nearly as doom-laden as the words husband and wife. If you have a best friend, he meets you in the street and says, with feigned surprise, "Oh, you are alive. Naturally, I thought you were dead as you didn't telephone me all of last week." And you think, "I could have phoned him, but what would I have said?" But they feel you owe it to them to stay in touch with them. And you forget to place yourself at the disposal of other people because you don't see any point in it, but this is wrong. If you are a friend, you have to see it from his point of view as well as your own. He clearly cares that you are no longer in his life.

There are no special men in my life either. Generally, I try not to regard one person above another. I think that is wrong. If we give more of our time, our money or our interest to one person rather than another, they will become the millionaires of love. And I come from a generation of people who wanted to redistribute the wealth of the world. So, to me, investing so much love in one person is to spend it unwisely. What then will happen to love's paupers? They should be our first concern: the unloved. So, there has never been a great love in my life. If there were, he would have to be somebody who was weaker, poorer and less equipped for life than I. So what kind of a man would he have been?

When I share the news of my perpetual singledom with people they say, "Aren't you lonely?" They fail to understand that people are only lonely if they don't know what to do with their time when they're alone. The lonely sit there thinking they are unloved, alone and of no use to the world. I, on the other hand, like to be alone because I feel I can rest and be my horrible self. You see, you have to be nice when you're with other people and it's a great strain. At least it is for me. So, I am very thankful when I get the chance to be by myself.

If you're alone and very glad of it, I wouldn't describe that as loneliness. I would describe that as solitude, which is a neutral word not carrying with it the idea of abandonment. It is simply a state of being by yourself. I've lived most of my life alone. I have a television set which I turn on, but if I didn't have it, I wouldn't miss it. I could go on alone without it because I would feel I was lucky that no disaster had ever overtaken me.

When the new towns were built in England, and they were put up in a few nights so that the families of factory workers could live there, all the women said, "I'm terribly lonely." I wondered, "Have they said to the people next door, 'I'm terribly lonely.'?" Because it seemed to me the problem of their loneliness could have been solved very easily.

I think that loneliness changes with age as well. When you are young, you are lonely because you have no friends. You don't know how to spend your time, so you feel you don't want to be alone. When you are young, it takes companions to energize you and make you happy. But that's the only time. I think only the young are lonely. For the rest of your life, you're glad to be alone.

There are lonely people in the world because they haven't learned to be alone. In some way they associate happiness with other people. I shouldn't think there are many lonely people in India, where you can be alone and meditate and all that. I should think lonely people only exist in the Western world. Such people make a grab at other people who don't want them, and then they feel rejected and more alone than ever.

Loneliness is also seen as a state absent of love. Now, I can't tell you anything about love. I would have said that love is the extra effort that we make in our dealings with those whom we do not like. And if, misguidedly, we are going to give more of our time, our interests and our money to one person rather than another, which you should not do, it should be given to the unlovable first.

There are a lot of people in the world who are not loved and we must make an inconspicuous dash to them to save them, to help them. To live a life and not be loved is a terrible thing. And we can spare them that if we are attentive.

Now, I don't really know when true love happens. But people are always telling me how they knew someone and weren't in love with them, and then they were in love with them, and then they weren't in love with them once more. I could never get at what they meant by 'being in love'.

Someone once said to me that they felt larger when they were in love, that they added the person to whom they loved to themselves and had a greater sort of life than they had before. That's some kind of an answer, but it's very difficult to define and I don't fully understand it. I've never felt anything like love for anybody, except that I love everybody, of course, but that, I think, is different.

A woman in England once said to me, "Everybody's the same to you." And I said, "No, they are all different, but they are all equal." I don't see how you can regard them any other way. Who are you to say that this person is better than that person? You don't have the right. So, I really can't believe in true love. I can't say it doesn't exist, but I've never experienced it and it has never been defined to me in a way which makes it understandable.

Regardless, I feel that true love is not needed. If you are sure of yourself, you do not need affirmation from another person. If you're with someone you can let them go. You can admire them and they can admire you. Do not make any demands of them. True love is a great mistake.

Having never been in love, I don't think I really know what it means. I understand fancying somebody, wishing somebody well, or enjoying someone's company, but what actually being in love is, I have no idea. Women become very angry when you say this. They say, "Of course you know what it is!" But I genuinely don't. Or they will say, "Well, you see things differently when you're in love." They put on a weird, affected voice when they say this, but I am still none the wiser. I would never alter my life to please another person. I alter my life to please people, plural, but not to please a single person.

When Ms. Streisand said, "The people who need people are the luckiest people in the world," she was being a very funny girl. Because the people who need people are badly off! But at least she meant people, not a person. And if you need people, there are always plenty of them around. Then if somebody drops out, someone else will take his place. I don't need any one person. I think it is a grave mistake to sit in your room wondering what some wretched man on another street is thinking about you. What does it matter? What matters is what you think about yourself.

When people say that they admire me, and that is very nice, I try not to take it for granted and I thank them and try to look amazed. But I think I would be worried if they loved me because, one assumes, they would then attempt to pursue me, which to me would be very embarrassing and difficult.

You won't be surprised to learn that I don't celebrate Valentine's Day. I do not buy Valentine cards and send them, signed or unsigned. I simply ignore the whole thing.

I have noticed that Valentine's Day is celebrated very differently on either side of the Atlantic, however. The British do it in such a way that it is a secret and with a great deal of coyness. A girl receives a card showing an arrow through a heart that includes a tender message. Everyone then says, "Oh! You have a secret admirer." She flutters her eyelids and she genuinely doesn't know who it's from. Of course, it may have been from her father or mother, but she doesn't know this unless she recognizes the handwriting. She looks at the postmark and it's sort of a game. Can one find out who her secret admirer is?

By contrast, Americans can't bear not to be

acknowledged, so they tell you the card is from them. In America, you receive signed Valentine cards, so you know exactly who your admirer is. To me this seems to take away some of the romance. Or at least it removes the element of fun.

When people know you are single and unloved, they assume you are lonely, and their next question is usually along the lines of, "Why don't you get yourself a cat or a dog?"

I don't like animals. Animals take up even more of your time than lovers. 'Animal' to me is a term of blame, as it was to the woman who wrote *His Hour* and *Three Weekends*[5]. In Glyn's books, the narrative will say something like, 'She flashed her inky pools of darkness at him. "Animal!" she hissed.'

I don't think people should have pets. Pets are substitutes for people. People are very proud to say, "I like animals more than people." This is a terrible confession: that they like that which they can rule, rather than that which they have to accommodate.

People say to me, "But you've never had a dog, have you?" And I say, "No." And they say, "Oh, you would think quite differently if you had. You don't understand. They love you unconditionally." I understand this perfectly well.

Owning a dog is to have the unconditional love of some wretched animal that barks, has to be taken out at seven in the morning in the snow and again at night, and has to have its poop cleaned away from the sidewalks when you venture out. They smell, they bark, they bite, they scratch, they jump, and what do they give you in return?

---

[5] Elinor Glyn, British romantic novelist.

Nothing. They should be left in the wild. They should be left to nature. I don't think we need animals in the world, except, perhaps, for food. In spite of what I regard as the obviousness of this, being American seems almost to require having a dog, but as I have said, this is a mistake.

Of course, the telephone is my friend. I am always surprised to hear so many men say of a holiday away from their homes, "At least I'm away from the 'phone." With what does the telephone threaten them? So many women never want to be a minute in a place where they cannot be reached by a telephone. It is their lifeline because women are talkers. Some of them even talk to their cat.

I, too, am a talker. And, of course, I should have been born a woman. Back in England, I was frequently accused of talking for talking's sake. What other reason, I asked, could anyone have for talking? If you speak merely to impart information, you are in trouble. There are only two kinds of information that can be imparted: what your hearer already knows, which is boring, or what he does not, which is humiliating.

Because I live alone I never speak from one day to the next unless the telephone rings. I suppose I could call someone, but to me that seems like a desperate measure. In addition, it would cost me money and, as I have said before, money is for saving not for spending. For that reason, I do not own an answering machine. Apart from the fact that I wouldn't know how to work it, it would mean that I might have to call people back. I can wait. I'm much happier waiting for them to call me again.

When I answer the telephone, I do so softly and slowly. A friend once described my voice as being like the opening of a coffin; all creaking and groaning. It isn't meant to be. It is intended to be cozy. It has been my experience that if people answer the telephone in a peremptory manner, their caller thinks, "I've called at a bad time." It is never a bad time to call me. I have been waiting. I try never to cut a conversation short, but if I must, I always particularize my excuse for doing so. If I merely say, "I'm just on my way out," my caller does not believe me. He immediately thinks I do not love him. Instead I say, "I am just going to LaGuardia Airport to meet a friend, who will be bewildered if I'm not there when he arrives." That, they believe.

All the same, I am aware that people call me to put me to the utmost test. The world seems to think that I am somehow boasting by having my number in the Manhattan telephone directory. They wish me to pay a terrible price for this, or else they think I am a fool for having my number listed.

Nevertheless, I feel it is my duty to have my number available to everybody. If I, who am only English, am allowed to live in America, where happiness rains down from the skies, what can I give in return? Since I cannot build a university or endow a hospital, I feel it is my duty to offer my infinite availability.

In Britain, everybody has his number in the London directory. I once looked for the number of the Westminster Library, wishing to ask them if they stocked a certain book so as to avoid going all the way there only to find that they didn't. Just above their number, my eye caught sight of an entry: *Westminster, Catherine Duchess of.* Well, I thought, if the Duchess of Westminster can have her number in the telephone book, then so can I. Besides, if you are not listed, you may well be stuck with your current friends. Now, I like my friends, but I'm mad about strangers.

I have no table in my room, so the telephone lies on the floor between my sole chair and the bed. That way it can be reached day or night. And people do call me late at night. Typically, the first thing such callers ask is, "Are you awake?" There are more unusual requests. A woman once called me at half past seven in the morning to ask me how to prevent her lipstick from blurring. My solution was flawless in its logic: "Never eat anything."

Another lady called to say that she had unwisely allowed her hairdresser to cut her hair very short and she now regretted it. What should she do? My answer was similar in nature to my previous advice: "Stay at home until it grows back to your preferred length."

While neither of these problems seemed urgent to me, they evidently were to the two women who contacted me. The thing that is hardest for me to understand is why some of my callers phone me without having decided what they are going to say. An apt conversation to highlight in this regard begins as follows:

STRANGER: Could I possibly speak to Mr. Crisp?
ME: This is me.
STRANGER: Oh. I didn't know that you would answer the phone yourself.
ME: Who did you think would answer it?
STRANGER: I don't know. . . . A secretary.
ME: At eleven at night?
STRANGER: I feel like a fool now.
ME: There's no need for that. I'm pleased to hear whatever it is you have to say.

This is not mere politeness. It's true on my part. People are my only hobby. I'm pleased to hear whatever anyone has to say. No one is boring to me, unless he says the same thing in the same way more than once in the same conversation. I once said that no one is boring who will talk about himself. For this statement the press laughed at me. So, now I say that no one is boring who will tell the truth about himself.

For when we say someone is boring it is in fact ourselves we criticize. We have not presented ourselves as a wide-open vessel into which a stranger feels he can pour anything. If someone is guarded in what he tells you, then he utters generalities. No one ever talks to me about the weather.

Very few calls I receive are hostile. When Mr. Letterman told the world in a television interview that my number was listed, I received perhaps half a dozen calls threatening my life over the next six months. I took them calmly, asking if each caller wanted to make an appointment. The volume was nothing compared to what I had received in the past. In England, I received half a dozen such calls a day.

Since I am not mechanically minded, and because of my great age, I am not teachable. As such, my telephone is of the old-fashioned dial variety and is wearing out. I know I will have difficulty acquiring a new one if it ever stops working. If it wears out before I do I may have to cease all telephonic communication entirely. That would make me very sad.

Without my phone I would miss out on the gossip of the world. I mean gossip in its original meaning here. Gossip used to mean idle talk about anything. Now it means malicious idle talk, which is a pity because it shows how far we've sunk as people. We don't idly talk about people, we speak maliciously about them. And that I think is bad.

I was horrified when, on the television program *Politically Incorrect*, a woman novelist - a biographer called Cathy Kelly - was accused by Mr. Maher[6] of printing

[6] Bill Maher, the host of *Politically Incorrect* from 1993 to 2002.

gossip. And a man who was also on the program said he thought it was a good idea that she wrote such books because it showed that the people we worshipped were no better than ourselves. I thought, "What a terrible thing that is to admit." I would never speak about other people and their failings. I repeat praise, but I never repeat blame.

I think the British gossip more than Americans. The English, who are so bent on those below them not entering their class, feel the need to defend themselves by saying nasty things about other people.

Of course, I have met unkind people throughout the world, and from time to time people have been unkind to me. When I was in San Francisco, I missed a meeting for the simple reason that I wasn't aware I was meant to attend. My agent hadn't told me. The papers said terrible things about me.

A woman, who I knew and thought was my friend, not only told me but cut out of the paper the clipping that said I was a terrible person and didn't keep my appointment. She gave it to me. I know if I had said to her, "Why have you done this?" She would have said, "I am your friend. Other people wouldn't tell you this, dear." But I think it was an unfriendly thing to do. I think she did it to have a hold over me. Sort of: "I am your friend, other people don't like you. Other people speak badly of you. I speak well of you. So now you belong to me."

Let me return to my aging telephone, if I may. When I tell people of my impending telephonic catastrophe, they tell me not to worry and claim that soon I will be using the Internet to communicate instead. This I am not looking forward to. I was told that the Internet would put me in touch with more than two million people. Well, as I can't cope with the people I am already in touch with, it doesn't seem much use.

Though I've been placed on the Internet, I can't tell what is happening to my world image, although at least I now realize that I have a world image. People tell me that they've seen or heard what I've said or done on the Internet.

I once said that I wanted to meet everybody in the world before I died. And nowadays everybody is thinking the same thing, because now they all own computers and each of these machines is connected to the Internet. I suppose that's nice. If we can all get in touch with more people, if we all know more people, we are less likely to be afraid of them and then we are less likely to attack them.

A word of warning however: if each of us can be in touch with the whole world now, we will all have to cling to our individuality more firmly than ever or else we risk getting lost in a sea of people.

In recent years I have been receiving email letters! I never know when I've received email letters, but when I ring up a man called Mr. Ward[7], who has a computer, he will tell me when I have email. His demon machine is what keeps me connected to the Internet.

The Internet seems to have made it easier for people to write to me. I tell him, "I can't write back to them all!" Instead, I think I will write my 'letter to the world', like Emily Dickinson[8]. Except that Ms. Dickinson's work begins, "This is my letter to the world, which never wrote to me." My letter will instead begin, "This is my letter to the world, which never stopped writing to me."

[7] Mr. Phillip Ward, co-editor of this book.

[8] Emily Elizabeth Dickinson was an American poet.

This is, as Ms. Dickinson would have said, my letter to the world, which never stopped writing to me. I was put on the Internet against my will, but I am very glad of the result of being put there. I like my friends, but I am mad about strangers. The only trouble is that I cannot reply to each of you separately. I can only thank you generally for the interest you have shown in me, in my work, and in my happiness.
Thank you.
Quentin Crisp

I was once asked if I thought the Internet was too abstract. I don't really. I don't think you can be too abstract because that is what gives things their poetry. Prose has to be matter of fact. Poetry doesn't. A woman I once knew wrote a poem which begins 'Once I was princess of this palace', and it goes on to describe 'a castle with cobwebs across its corridors' and stairs. In the poem she is wandering through it when there is a door, which is locked. She wrote and said to me, "I don't know what to say is behind the door." And I said, "Don't say anything." The last line of her poem is 'Time now to turn to that locked door'. That's what you have to do with poetry, leave it open-ended.

Of course, the modern trend is to look for sex on the Internet. I think that's a dubious proposition. I think sex is better if it springs from a contact. I can't describe how I think affairs should begin, but they should begin pretty soon after you meet someone. Because you can easily get to know someone so well that you can't possibly have an affair with them. There comes a time when you know them well enough to have an affair with them, but not too well. But seeking a sexual partner on the Internet, I think, is very unwise. So, the whole Internet may just be a mistake. It's bound to all just be about sex in the end.

5. PEOPLE WHO WORK

Work is a terrible thing. I presume somebody has to do it. And once you do it, you're stuck with it. I can't imagine. I think you should avoid work, if you can. But if you can't, you have to find a job where you can add what you are to what you do. That is the essence. But if you can avoid it, avoid it.

The secret of looking young is, of course, never, never work, and this I really believe in. I was asked this secret by Mr. Rose, and I said, "Never, never work." He laughed nervously, so I think it was not the answer he was looking for. But, of course, it's work that makes you look old because you have to get up at half past seven every morning and leave the house by half past eight, and get to the office by half past nine. Also, it's the look of resentment that settles on to your face when you begin to think, "Why do I have to work for them?" And that makes you look even older.

If you hate your job, I think you should leave it. But I don't think you should leave it suddenly and I don't think you should leave it and say you hated it. That gives the impression that the job was badly presented to you or that you worked with people you didn't like. And I don't think you should ever portray not liking anyone. So, when you get a better job, you say that you have to go and that you are very sorry and that you had a wonderful time, but now you have a job nearer home or one that pays more or something of that nature. That's if you're even asked why you're leaving. You may not be asked. You may go to your boss and say, "I'm leaving." And he may say, "Well, thank God for that."

When I left one firm of printers, the foreman said, "Oh, thank God. I was wondering what we were going to do with you." I worked in the art department and it was a thankless job because the price of the artwork was always reduced and then reduced further until the firm finally got the order for the printing. But, as an artist, you still had to try and make your wages. And, of course, you couldn't do that because you were charging less and less. Somehow I survived. I was there for four years in the end.

I've never worked in America at all. In America, you see - and I didn't know this until I got here - you can just do fame. It's what I call the 'profession of being' and that is how I have earned a living. Chiefly, I have relied on the kindness of strangers. If you don't yet know that you can do this, you should blame your mother. Mothers spend their lives saying, "Well, you'd better learn because you'll be alone and people won't help you." This is a lie. People will help you. But in order to best receive their help, it's advantageous to look as helpless as you can.

I remember standing at a bus stop once and a taxi drove up and said, "Get in and I'll take you as far as we go." Sensing that he didn't mean to charge me, I got in. And we drove a great long distance and, to his word, he didn't charge me a penny. A woman I once told this story to said, "They've never done that for me." To which I inquired, "Do you try and look helpless?" And she said,

"No! Of course, I don't." Well, if you don't look helpless how are you ever going to get help?

In my case I don't even need to look helpless. I am helpless. I am neither proud nor ashamed of this fact. For other people it is problematic. They neither want to appear nor be helpless. They prefer to be in control and independent from the world. I avoid both of these things. I do try and resist being cute, however. I worry when I'm told I am cute. I don't like the word. I think being cute is an endeavor to make use of being undersized. Anyway, I try to resist it because I know that in the end it's not cute, it's annoying.

I do not consider writing to be work. Mr. Bolden once said that he had met only two people who said they liked writing and he didn't believe either of them. I once met the literary critic of the *Financial Times* at a bus stop, and he said, "Do you like writing?" I said, "No. Good heavens." He continued, "I love it, but then I'm a born lighthouse-keeper."

If you are a born lighthouse-keeper, of course you love writing. You'd be happy to sit alone in a lighthouse ignoring the world. Personally, I dread the day when I will have to say, "I can't come out to play, I haven't done my homework." I hope that day will never come.

I think I've lived my life 'in excess in moderation'. 'Excess in moderation' is a lovely state because you have what is an excess to other people, but is in moderation to yourself. Almost everything you do is excessive to other people. They will always say, "Why do you do this? What makes you do that?" And usually they are referring to things that are second nature to me. I find that I can't reply. I've never thought about why I do certain things, but I should. A person should know why they do everything. As the saying goes, the unexamined life is not worth living.

But I have never gone so far in any one direction as to destroy other people or even to worry them very much. I expect my mother was worried about what would happen to me, but I reassured her that I would be alright; and during her life, I was. I don't think anyone else has cared enough about me to think, "Oh, I don't think he should do that. He'll go too far. He'll get put in prison. He'll make himself ill." Or indeed say anything.

Although I think I have lived my life in moderation, I have indulged myself in the matter of time. I live without most things, but with lots and lots of time. Most people don't have enough time and they complain about it, especially women, who now have several jobs to do at once. To be a mother, to be a housekeeper, to be a cook, and to go to the office and type. I mean, it's a life they've chosen, mostly. Or else it is a life their husband has chosen for them because he took a job that made it necessary for both of them to work in order to maintain their standard of living.

Everyone is mad about their standard of living these days. It's very difficult for a man to say, "Let's live more cheaply. Let's go live in a poorer part of town and not worry about the neighbors and not have a car." All so that he needn't work so hard. I can't imagine a man saying that, but if he did it would be wonderful because women are the people who suffer for this craze about the standard of living. Men always say when challenged, "I've done it all for you and the children." But, of course, they haven't. They've done it for themselves.

Now, when it comes to my standard of living, I wanted to get as low as possible. To have nothing. That way, nothing could be taken from me. So, I lived my life wanting nothing and wanting to have nothing. And now I want nothing and I have nothing, so I suppose I have succeeded in this quest. I don't put material value on anything. Actually, that's not quite true, because I care about almost everything in this room, and I would be very worried to lose any of it. But this room is tiny, so I hope I cannot be faulted for that. So, I do care about material things, but not on a very large scale. I'm a very bad example of materialism and consumerism. I don't want to have a car, because I can't drive. I don't want a large house, because I couldn't look after it. In a perfect world, I would like to have endless money and no possessions, because if you have endless money you have endless power. And if you have no possessions, you have no worries. So, power without any feelings of guilt. That seems to me to be an ideal state.

In spite of my lack of observable wealth, I don't think there has ever been a time in my life when I've gone without eating or without comfort. I don't think I've ever realized that until now.

Back to my previous statement, about power without guilt, I should make it clear that, personally, I reject any personal attainment of power. I never take a superior position in any relationship with people. Instead, I consider myself the slave and as a result I am not to blame for anything. If you assume command, then you are to blame.

It was of course writing that led me to the profession of being. I hesitate here to use the word 'famous', since I am nothing and I am no one. But it was Mr. Greene[9], I believe, who said he couldn't expect more than 250 usable words to be written each time he sat down to write. So, he probably wrote a great many and then felt that a small portion of what he wrote could be used. He put them together and that constituted his work for the day. Now

[9] Henry Graham Greene, English novelist

that's very little. I would have expected a productive day to consist of about twice that, or to have at least two pages of presentable type. That at least is my experience. I mean, you wouldn't get far with a narrative in only 250 words. To write a book, in my experience, you should write about 1000 words a day. That way, by the end of the year you'll have finished your book.

Mr. Styron[10] said it took him six years to write *Sophie's Choice*. Now I don't think he meant he sat down in a hut at the end of the garden every day for six years until it was complete. He wrote it and then he forgot about it. Then he wrote other things. Then he went on holiday. And then finally he went back to it. What he meant was it took six years from writing the first sentence to completing the last. Doubtless he probably scrapped what he had written more than once or twice and began writing again.

I could never take that long. Not because I write faster or better, but because my patience is limited. If it took that long I would get tired of it and think, "Oh, this is no good. I should give this up!" When I sat down to write *Love Made Easy*, I was determined to get it done in about six months. And that's quite different from six years.

To my mind, the best way to write is to write about yourself. You pick a beginning someplace or sometime that interests you and you go from there. When you want to describe how you hated your parents, you describe them and it will go somewhere in the book. I don't think most people can begin at the beginning and end at the end. I think they have to write about what interests them and then join it all together. Because you are writing your autobiography, that gives you the shape of the book. Time

---

[10] William Styron Jr., American novelist

is the skeleton onto which you add the flesh. So, you know that, when you've written about your childhood, you then write about your adolescence. Then you write about being a young man and so on.

If you're writing a novel, you don't use that same skeleton. So, you are more or less at sea. And I don't know how people write novels. I have written one novel, *Chog*, a satirical novel about the welfare state. The whole thing was planned before I started, and then I truly did begin at the beginning. I don't think there's any secret about writing a novel, but then I've never written an important book.

The fact that I love words helped me write. I don't know why I love words so much. I think that you have to first of all govern yourself with the use of them. You cannot go on the stage and seize at the first word and make it a sort of theme. You have to decide what adjectives to use. You're not allowed to have your favorite adjective. And that's very important. You must think, "Do I mean fabulous? Do I mean part of a fable? Marvelous? Do I mean that which causes me to marvel, to wonder about the origin of this phenomenon?"

You see, people use all the words which intensify their adjective. And that is very bad. You can't say, "Terribly good." For a thing to be terrible, it should frighten you. You have to think about what you're saying. Most people use clichés like 'crystal clear'. Clear is quite enough without prefixing it with crystal. You can't say "very" over and over again, because that really intensifies the adjective that it comes before. You have to express what you're saying in other words.

The word I use the most is the word 'kinky'. This is because it describes anything which is a variant on the expected, the normal, the conventional and the average. I use it a great deal because it saves me the trouble of saying 'perverse'. Well, perhaps not 'perverse' but certainly 'eccentric'. I once caught myself saying 'kinky' at least six times in one afternoon. I am sure other people describe me as kinky. I don't think I have a least favorite word. I like all words.

Of course, I had two brothers who were educated not at the same school, but at similar schools, and who had the same upbringing and the same parents that I did. They didn't cling to words in the same way as I did. I remember when I was young saying of condensed milk "It's a glutinous substance." And my nanny said, "Oh, where did you learn that word?" I dismissively and snobbishly thought, "You fool." So, from a very early age, I clung to words, not because they made me seem educated or grown up, but simply because I liked that they described a situation or a thing so precisely or perfectly. The power of words was what I liked. I had liked words even before I could spell them.

From all of that it's now obvious to me why I went into the profession of writing and speaking. Words are my friends. And if you can surround yourself with friends and indeed do something that you love, you will, as the saying goes, never do a day's work in your life.

6. FLAPPER GIRLS AND WALT DISNEY

I don't think there was a decade I recognize that had as long a lasting individuality like the 1920s. The Twenties came immediately after the First World War, which was the first time in a long time that the English realized that everything in the world was not plain sailing. It was the first time in living memory that the British thought they might not be destined to rule the world.

Noel Coward spoke of this in his play - later an award-winning film - *Cavalcade.* One of his characters sits at the piano, waving an ostrich feather, singing, "Who's escaped those weary twentieth century blues?" It was a descriptive song about the decadence of the world. As far as I'm concerned, the 1920s was the most noticeable decade, the most stylish in which I have lived.

After the war, which ended in 1918, everything changed. It was known that right would not always win out over wrong. Not without cost, anyway. It was known that war was a terrible thing. It was known that heartbreak was everywhere and there was a change in the human psyche. It was that change that gave the next decade its desperation. Everybody went mad and sex reared its ugly head in public after decades of being swept under the carpet.

I was born in 1908, of course, so in 1910 I was only two, and in 1920 I was only twelve, but I do remember what the fashions were like. I remember my mother saying, "When we look back at the photographs that are being taken, we shall think we went mad." So, the fashions seemed extreme even to a middle-class suburban woman like my mother. I wonder if my older sister was a flapper girl. You see, to be a flapper meant you were brazen. It meant you went out and displayed yourself in a way that I don't think women had displayed themselves before that.

The flappers didn't affect me because, of course, I was only ten. But they wore incredibly short skirts. *Punch* was full of jokes about some racy young girl shocking her uncle by saying things that now seem perfectly normal, but which back then seemed so shocking. There seemed to be a resurgence in the importance and the worship of youth that had hitherto been absent. You see, in 1910, the world was ruled by middle-aged people. But by 1920 it was ruled by young people, much as it is today.

There was a great change in art as well. In 1926, the Surrealists had an exhibition in England. Of course, by that time surrealism had existed in France for years. But it hadn't existed in England and everybody had to try and adapt themselves to this confusing idea that pictures were not representations of nature; they were something else. And I should think that Ms. Stein's[11] writing began in the Twenties. I can't remember when precisely she flourished, but I have a feeling it would have been in the Twenties. During that time, all Americans went to Paris. Anita Loos[12] said Paris is where good Americans go when they die. And

[11] Gertrude Stein, American novelist, playwright and poet.

[12] Anita Loos, American screenwriter, playwright and author.

back then, Parisians loved Americans. Now it's very different. America's subsequent domination of international affairs and France's own waning influence has meant that the average Frenchman now loathes Americans, which is a great shame.

Women stopped being 'ladies' after the First World War, though for a while society held them to its previous standards. Consequently, if you wore a short skirt and danced the Charleston, people would judge you and say you were going to hell. Part of being a lady, in the traditional sense, is to be discreet and modest, and women of the 1920s lost both of those qualities.

In 1926, skirts were so short that they were above the knee. Prior to that, I don't think anyone had ever seen a woman's knee. Perhaps they thought they didn't even have them. The discovery was certainly shocking. There were, of course, endless comments about it in magazines. About women wearing makeup, and whether or not it was acceptable for them to be seen applying it in public. It was as if it was acceptable so long as people didn't see the act of application. That way, a woman's look could be thought of as either natural, which is absurd, or else one that didn't involve effort, which is just naïve.

Of course, it was men who wrote the magazines back then as well, so the articles were obviously one-sided. Men were feeling lost, absent of a female class that they could respect. It must have been quite difficult. With conversations about sex taking place in ordinary society, how far could a man go in talking about sex? Previously, two of the greatest taboos of English society were sex and money, and up until then a gentleman knew that neither topic was a subject for public conversation.

Men continued to dress in the same way as previously and this, of course, meant that women complained that men wore boring clothes and that every man was a clone. They were to an extent. They all wore clothes that were all exactly alike: double-breasted suits and wide trousers. Trousers that covered your feet and went as far forward as your toes. They were called spats. My father wore spats - I suppose because everyone else did. The general logic was that they either kept you warm or else kept your socks clean. I don't know. And almost all men wore hats when they went to work.

Of course, I never wore a hat. I remember someone saying to me once, "Oh, you're part of the hatless brigade." It was not meant as a compliment. Back then it had never occurred to me to wear a hat. These days people don't even recognize me without one. My attitude these days is one of practicality, however. I wear a hat principally so that my head won't be cold and my hair won't be ruffled.

Back then men wore hats with no hair visible south of the hat's brim. The back of a man's head had to be trimmed. I remember visiting the barber with my mother and receiving the haircut that was assigned to me. I could feel the clippers going "Bbllrrr! Bbllrrr! Bbllrrr!" It must have been thought untidy or even dirty to have a lot of hair hanging about. Long hair on a man would have been considered disheveled.

I longed to have long hair. I remember when I was twenty, after I had left home to live on my own, visiting a barber in High Wycombe and saying, "Could I have hair like Jesus Christ?" And the barber said, "I have never had the privilege of cutting that gentleman's hair." Which was both a marvelous response and also a way of telling me that I was making a grave error in judgement.

Although Queen Victoria died in 1901, she sort of laid the groundwork for the change that permeated womanhood in the 1920s. She was a kind of trendsetter for fashion. She introduced all sorts of things that previously had been considered vulgar. She wore rings on all her fingers, including her thumbs. Everyone behaved very well in her presence and everyone longed to be like her.

Another change that took place during that decade concerned women's role during sex. In England, before the 1920s, sex was considered a burden that women had to bear, rather than a pleasure. I get the feeling that for many women it still is. And back then the only reason for sex was to produce heirs and offspring. But, of course, no one ever mentioned it. Even these days we only hear about the bold people. The wild people. The actresses. I'm sure most people's sex lives are still dull and full of duty. So, perhaps things have not really changed all that much.

I hate to think what my parents' sex life was like. If it mirrored their marriage it would have been cold and stale. Of course, one's principal reference point for marriage is one's parents. Theirs is the relationship to which we are most exposed when we are young and impressionable. In my case, my mother and father hated one another, though they never raised their voices in front of us. It didn't deceive me, or anyone else, into thinking they were happy, but I think that was meant to be the idea. Anyway, I knew that marriage was no good from an early age.

Even so, my brothers and sister got married, and they were just as much exposed to my parents as I was. My sister in particular must have had an odd view of marriage. After five years she went to a doctor and asked why she was not yet pregnant, to which he replied, "Because you are still a virgin." So goodness knows what, if anything, they had been doing. How she didn't know what sex was, let alone how a woman actually becomes pregnant, I have no idea. But it definitely wasn't part of the school curriculum back then and she did, of course, marry a clergyman.

He should have known what was going on, of course. The bible is full of sex and rape. I can only assume she didn't consult with him before visiting the doctor, because surely he would have set her straight. Anyway, things must have changed because she did get pregnant in the end, and she ended up giving birth to a daughter. That must have been an awkward conversation however. Either he wasn't physically interested in her or he was just as naïve as she was. I find that hard to believe though. Anyway, they ended up having just the one child, so either they went back to doing whatever it was they did before, or else one or both of them decided it wasn't worth all the effort or embarrassment.

My sister must have had a strange life - not that she ever discussed it with me or, I think, anybody. But she did tell one of her nieces the story of her being a virgin after five years of marriage. Otherwise we would never have known, because I never would have thought about it or questioned it.

Although the awakening of female youth that occurred in the 1920s calmed down a little in the immediate decades that followed, the changes that it ushered in have remained more or less to the present day. These days, women have abandoned being ladies. Most have abandoned being women, which is a pity. They have instead decided to be people, which is a terrible thing because that's settling downward. Equality is all very well, but that doesn't mean that men and women have to behave the same as each other.

Back then, women were nicer than people. Now they go to work, which I suppose they have to now that everything is so expensive. If you have a house and two children these days, your husband's wages are not enough, which is very sad. Likewise, men can no longer be gentlemen because their role and earnings potential seem to have changed. And while I can see that being a lady or a gentleman is now outdated and unreasonable, I do miss it. Chiefly I miss ladies, because they were such spectacularly feminine creatures. Of course, gentlemen were only gentlemen in public. They were rats when no one was looking. But both are now extinct. Fatalities of modern living.

The 1920s was also the decade that brought Walt Disney to the world, with his now famous mouse first appearing in 1928. I remember seeing the original Disney cartoons, which were short films lasting about eight minutes, part of a program that included a double-feature and had various shorts as well.

In those days, a trip to the cinema was really wonderful because you were in the dark for about three and a half hours. You saw two films, a main feature and a B-feature, which lasted about an hour, then you had a travelogue, which was boring, but then you saw a lacquer cartoon which was usually one of Mr. Disney's.

I remember the first time I saw Mickey Mouse, and I instantly liked him. He was better than Felix the Cat, the star of another cartoon series, because he was so much livelier. So, I loved Mickey Mouse and all of his friends, but people criticized him. Well, not so much him but his creators and producers. They thought his cartoons were too violent. I didn't mind the violence. I liked the movement and the comedy. I thought they were wonderful films. Unfortunately, now, 'Disney' has become a term that has come to mean a sentimentalization of serious subjects, which is a pity. People use the phrase 'disneyfied' to mean something which has had all the bite taken out of it, something that has been made sweet and charming and bland and innocent.

Times Square is one of the places that they claim has been disneyfied. Times Square used to be such a wonderful place. I remember saying to a friend of mine when the peepshow houses were shut down, "If you can't go to hell in your own way, what good is life?" To which he replied, "Yes! And if you can't go to Hell in your own way in New York, where can you?"

After his original shorts Mr. Disney went on to make feature-length cartoon films, the first of which I saw was *Snow White*. I think I saw most of them, in fact. As a designer by trade, I could see the artistry in what he did. I remember seeing a documentary about him, in which he took you inside his film studios and showed you the making of a cartoon film. That was marvelous. When he had a unit in England, I tried to be part of it but they wouldn't have me. And I remember coming home from an interview there, broken and disillusioned. But that was back when I was trying to be a designer, when I thought I had to work to earn a living - long before I learned you could come to America and do fame instead.

An interviewer once asked me if I'd thought about having a Disney cartoon based on me. I don't know why they asked me that. I mean, I would love it, but what could he show me doing or being? I don't think you could have a story about me that was clean enough to appeal to Mr. Disney's fans. Of course, all the great film stars were at one time or another characters in one of his films. Ms. Hepburn[13] even played Bo Peep in one of them. I would have liked to voice a character in one of Mr. Disney's films. That would have made me immortal.

[13] Audrey Hepburn, British actress and model

7. THE RELIGIOUS RIGHT

The Religious Right is the biggest mistake I can think of, but I don't think you can alter people's religious views without creating a lot of trouble. This is because, generally, people don't want their religion tampered or interfered with. I don't know where they got their views from, but I think it may have been from St. Paul, who was the public relations officer of the whole 'sin movement'. Christ, of course, said almost nothing about sin or sex, except that if you looked at a woman with desire you had already committed adultery.

St. Paul on the other hand had very definite views about sin. He said it was better to marry than to burn. Which is not a hearty recommendation for the state of matrimony, but does give you the impression that he thought casual sex was wrong. I think that is the stumbling block most people have with the Religious Right. They don't want people to be happy, except in a conventional married setting. And that has to change, but I don't know how.

The Religious Right, like most other religious people, have the view that everyone has to think the same way. Generally, I think that's a view that all people have. We all think we are right, that we know best and that we have it all figured out. Conversely, if you do not have the same moral system as someone else, you're wrong in their eyes and will have to change your mind.

Nonbelievers have a looser view. I have never known a nonbeliever who was angry about the people who did believe. Not solely on the basis of their belief, anyway. It's the believers who are angry with people who don't believe, so there's something wrong with the believers. It's insecurity of the highest order.

Yet, though I can identify that as the chief problem, I don't think we can alter it in our own lifetime. I don't think it's part of human nature to accept that other people have a different belief and they must be allowed to maintain it. We all want to be right and, when confronted with someone who thinks otherwise, we take it as an affront or a challenge to our own beliefs.

In truth, there never can be a total divorce between church and state, even though it is written into the U.S. Constitution. This is because whatever people do has a moral value, whether it is a political act or a personal act or an attitude. And if you can bring the moral value into it, then it becomes a religious question. So it's unrealistic to think you can divorce church from state. You can, of course, divorce them inasmuch as you can avoid invoking a formal religion, but religion will always find its way into politics, not least because it's the puritans and missionaries who tend to stand for office.

Everything has a moral value, but in truth morality is expediency in a long white dress. When Moses said to the Jews, "Thou shalt not kill," what he wanted to preserve was their number. When he took the Jews out of Egypt, they weren't fighters. They were waiters and actors. They were anybody. And he was taking them across extremely hostile terrain, a long journey over the desert. Yet, round the other side of every sand dune was a band of desert fighters: the Malachites and the Hittites for example. And the only weapon that the Israelites had was their number. If they were seen to be a huge band of people, no one would attack them. So, Moses realized that, if they fought among themselves, they would lose as a band of people. He knew you can't carry a wounded man through the desert; you would have to leave him behind.

So, the rules he 'received' were convenient to his predicament. You mustn't kill people. You mustn't steal from people because that leads to trouble. You mustn't insult your parents because that causes ill-feeling. He wanted it all to be kept smooth so that the Israelites' numbers would never decrease. So, when he came down from the mountain[14], he knew he couldn't say, "I have decided thou shalt not kill" because that would lead to them saying, "And who are you?" So, he adopted the American solution, he said, "My agent says thou shall not kill." And his agent was God. And that's how he got away with it.

One of the odd things about the Religious Right is, of course, their affinity for guns. It doesn't seem to tie in to the 'thou shalt not kill' theme discussed above. In my opinion there are too many guns in America. And in truth there are just as many opinions about guns in America as there are actual guns. I just don't think guns are necessary. I don't understand why Mr. Heston[15], who of course once famously played Moses in a motion picture, says that they

[14] With the Ten Commandments

[15] Charlton Heston, an American actor and five-term president of the National Rifle Association

are. Mr. Heston says that Americans have the right to bear arms and this, of course, is true. But it's a nonsense rule, because it is a frontiersman rule. There are no frontiers now. Nobody now goes out onto a wooden porch with a shotgun and says to an unknown visitor, "What do you want?" I mean, nowadays we all live civilized lives. We don't need guns. You call at the house, you are invited in and you sit down and talk.

I think the fascination with guns is connected to the American dream of manliness, which obsesses American males. Females too. They obsess about the sexes. Women should be feminine and a man should be manly. They've occasionally gotten the women to be feminine, but they haven't gotten the men to be fully manly. Men will go to gymnasiums and build up their muscles until they look quite strange, but they never do anything with them except display them. So, really that's no help.

In America, because of the guns, there are a colossal number of shootings. Murders. We hear about them because we live in the age of television. In a time gone by, with no television, it would be years before you heard that there had been a murder in Portland, Oregon. And then you'd think, "I never heard about that. Oh, I wonder what happened." But now we hear about everything, all the time, as it's happening. That's probably a good thing because we now know what a terrible state we're in.

In England, if you had a television show with a plot that involved a wife shooting her husband, thinking him to be a burglar, you would have to explain why there was a gun in the house. The husband, before he was shot, would have to say something like, "I have bought my wife a gun because we live 500 yards from the nearest house, and we've already been robbed twice." But in America, she would hear cool padded feet on the stairs, she would lean out of bed and take from the bottom drawer of a bedside cupboard a gun. You wouldn't see her load it. You wouldn't see her remove the safety catch. And we would accept that she knows how to use it and effortlessly shoots the intruder dead. No other explanation is needed in America. That's the right to bear arms.

Of course, criminals will obtain guns whether they are legal or not. Based on this, the pro-gun lobby argues that it would only be law-abiding citizens that would suffer from gun control or an outright ban. But I can't help thinking that, if only the police and criminals had arms, we would be a bit better off because right now all children are gangsters and they shoot people indiscriminately. It's pretty frightening.

The latest school shooting[16], at Columbine High School, which is currently receiving blanket coverage on television, was very surprising. The perpetrators were apparently planning it for a long time and that makes it really very sinister. That you get hold of your best friend and you say, "Let's shoot them up." If I had possessed a gun at school, I would certainly have shot everybody. Chiefly the staff. But I didn't have a gun and it would have been very difficult for me to get one. It's so easy for people to get guns these days in America. Guns lie about the houses of people where there are children. Or children know where the guns are stored and can get at them.

People worry about the effect on children of television, but no one faces the real issue. Why do you make toy guns? Why not forbid them to be made? If children didn't see them in shops, within six months they wouldn't want them. And these days manufacturers make toy guns that are long

---

[16] April 20, 1999

and hyper-realistic. The kids all want them and then they run around 'shooting' everybody with them. It's not a stretch to see why they then go and shoot people with real guns. Another tragedy is when children point the toy guns at the police, who think they are real, and get shot for real themselves. All you have to do is forbid the making of toy guns.

I can understand the disasters of the world if they are unforeseeable or unforgettable, but when things are so easy to prevent and are still not done, it's incomprehensible to me. Currently, to an American child, to be grown up is to carry a gun. You have to alter that, which only takes a little arrangement. I don't know if there's much money to be made out of selling toy guns, but I don't think money should be made this way. I don't think money or profit should be the sole reason for anything.

So, it's all so strange, but I have a very calm view of life. I've never been in a street where there's been a shooting, and I walk about the streets quite a lot on the Lower East Side. In fact, I've never been in any danger of any kind. I have never lived in a house where I suddenly heard two loud bangs and went out of my room and found someone lying in the corridor, dead. In fact, I've never seen anyone who is dead.

A more understandable position of the Religious Right is their pro-life stance. When I say, more understandable, I don't mean that I agree with it. Just that it seems more in keeping with their narrow view of the world.

When I made the terrible mistake of saying that, if a woman was pregnant and had a child which had a gay gene, she was justified in aborting the fetus, my agent, Ms. Clausen said, "What a terrible thing to say! Would your mother, if she had known you were going to be gay, have aborted you?" Well, of course, the question is absurd because we lived in the suburbs at a time when no one had an abortion. So I said as much. In 1908, when I was born, the only people who had abortions were those who became pregnant and were unmarried. In that instance they simply went away to have some unmentionable illness cured. Of course, really they were having an abortion.

My mother would never have had an abortion, but if she had known the trouble I was going to be, she would have done anything to prevent me from being born. All the screaming matches with my father, the squabbles with my brothers and sister and their hatred toward me, the weeping and wailing and the carrying on. She certainly would not have had me if it could have been avoided. But you see, no one knew any of that when I was sufficiently unformed to be safely aborted.

And now we have fertility drugs to help make even more children! I think we need to preempt the next crisis by making contraception available to everybody, because as far as I can see we're heading towards a potentially insurmountable problem of overpopulation. If the population doubles in the next twenty-five years, we shall all be standing on the shore with our feet pointing to the sea because there won't be any room. So we have got to think of ways to reduce this future burden on the earth and on mankind.

Now, I do like the Pope[17]. I think he looks nice and that he looks papal. And I love his gestures and the way he holds his hands out so that they are like little wings. But I don't know why he encourages people to have more children, especially in places like South America and

[17] Pope John Paul II

Mexico where the population is increasing so fast that no one can cope with it. But, I suppose, he doesn't know what else to say that is within the teachings of Christianity. Abortion didn't exist when Christ was alive, so he didn't have any opinions about that. If he had, I don't think he would have said that everyone should have children.

The problem is that more children means more families and more strife, though this is principally the fault of another failed viewpoint of the Religious Right, namely that of family values: the notion that the family unit should be the center of the universe and the sole concern of every family member. In my experience it's the surest way to unhappiness.

Since I became a sort of mail-order guru, by which I mean since people started writing to me with their problems, seeking my counsel on what they should do, I have come to the opinion that all human beings should live alone. It is the only way to avoid conflict in your life and live a truly harmonious life. All of the problems I hear about involve a husband, lodger, father, mother, daughter or brother. Which is to say that all life's problems involve the people you live with.

So, the solution to human unhappiness is for everybody to live alone, but, of course, that's very expensive. So, instead, people live together in the same way that students live, six in an apartment. They manage somehow to get on for a while until finally their age overtakes them and they walk out.

It's obvious to me that people do not get on very well if they see too much of one another. All the murders nowadays are murders within a family. Parents murder their children. Children murder their parents. Husbands murder their wives, and so on. It's very seldom that you hear of one stranger murdering another stranger.

The misguided focus on the family unit is especially damaging to mothers, who waste almost the entirety of their lives fussing over their offspring. One doesn't realize as a child, but mothers never talk about anything except their children. As a child you think, "Oh! I never get out, from under my mother. She's always telling me what to do. She's telling me what to wear. She's telling me what to say." It never dawns on you that she actually thinks of nothing but you.

When I was an artists' model, I occasionally worked in what I have called 'housewives' choice classes'. In other words, classes for middle-aged women who've got through the housework in record time and have time left over to go to art school.

The conversation during the rest period of such classes was always about children. Never about themselves. They would ask each other, "How is your youngest daughter?" "Oh, my youngest daughter's alright. She's got her head screwed on. It's my eldest daughter I'm worried about. She's now got another young man. I haven't dared to show him to Herbert. He's got a beard!"

When I lived for a time in the Algonquin, there was nothing for me to do in the time I had off from my one-man show. So, I used to lie on my bed and watch television. Every program began thus: "I'm worried about Paul. I don't think Hillary is right for him." There would be some filler and some action, but at the end of every episode, at least three people were in the hospital, either poisoned, pregnant, self-harmed or shot. No one ever said, "Do you not think perhaps it is time we stopped meddling in the lives of others?" I watched and waited for those words to be said. They never came.

In my lifetime I must have known at least one hundred and fifty women well enough for them to tell me their life story. And when I meet them in the street, before they've said hello, they inevitably tell me, "What do you think he did today?" or "What do you think he's done now?" People need to ditch the notion that they must get married and raise a family in order to lead a good or worthwhile life. The idea that a family unit is the ideal model for living life is a fallacy. It's a mistake.

Yes, many years ago, if you didn't get married and you instead ended up living at home and looking after your increasingly aged and cantankerous mother and father, you were considered to have had a rotten life. But that is not the only alternative to matrimony these days. Nowadays, living alone is not only a viable option, but the best way to ensure your own happiness. A happiness free of the burden of other people.

8. AMERICANS

My favorite country is, of course, America. This is not just because I can't speak another language, but rather because America is my home and the place for doing fame. Generally though, English people do not learn foreign languages. They go abroad and if they're not immediately understood they simply speak louder. And this, if anything, can only make us harder to understand rather than easier. But this fact doesn't deter us.

I've never seen Europe. Americans think that England is part of Europe. The English disagree. They see themselves as English and those people across the English Channel are 'Continentals'. Typically, the English don't have a good word to say about any nation other than their own. The French are sex maniacs. The Italians are dirty. The Germans are warmongers. The Welsh are thieves. The Irish are drunkards. The Scottish are mean. Americans are overbearing. Only the English are right. Obviously I do not share these xenophobic viewpoints. It is my ambition to meet everyone in the world, as I have said. Even if I can't understand them, I bear them no ill will.

I think the people in America are very nice, and sometimes I wonder why that is. I think the answer is that no one in America is ashamed of being of service. In England, it's an issue. If an Englishman takes a menial or demeaning job to make some more money, they feel the need to laugh it off. But Americans freely get jobs in hotels and restaurants and they say, "I am doing it to earn some more money." And they don't feel they have to explain it in any other way.

I also think America is a very feminine country. By contrast I found England a masculine country. You see, England was a very small place full of people so the movement was outward, and when they landed in foreign countries and met the unfortunate locals the English said, "These are the crops you will grow. These are the gods you will worship. Now go and do it." It's a very masculine thing to do and say, to naturally think that you are right and to direct others to do your bidding.

But America was, at least initially, a huge place with nobody in it. So, the movement was inward. When immigrants came up from below deck, they would be processed and accepted. Then, when they were offered work, whatever it was, they said, "I'll do it. What is it?" Because they regarded anything they could be asked to do as being better than what they had in Europe. And that is what gave America its national characteristic of an eagerness to please.

But something is changing in America now. When I was young, the caricature of Americans was one of boastfulness. Now Americans are apologetic, and that's very sad. You see, back then everybody owed money to America. Now America owes money to everybody. What has gone wrong? We should be a nation of millionaires. I don't know why it is that it's happened, and if I knew I would seek to undo it. But now Americans have been made to doubt themselves by other countries, which is a pity.

I do not find Americans greedy. I think they are slightly more materialistic, but that's only because they openly show their materialism. I think the English are just as materialistic, but of course in England there is nothing to covet. There are no great tracts of land over there about which you can fight a war.

You see, there was a man called Mr. Monroe[18], and he believed that the Americas, North and South, could exist independently of the world. That was, of course, before Americans developed a taste for automobiles and a thirst for gasoline. Now I don't pretend to understand world events, but I imagine that now America has to be nice to certain Middle-Eastern countries to get the oil it requires, and that has in turn made the Middle-Eastern countries sneer at us.

The least likable quality of Americans is the way they bother other people. I mean this on an international scale. You see, when the Vietnam War was on, I said to Ms. Page[19], "Why didn't they go out there, measure the place up, send back for a bomb and drop it?" And she said, "So that's alright for the Vietnamese, is it?" Well, it would have been alright for the Vietnamese because fewer of the brave and the beautiful would have died. To me that would be no worse than all those people dying in a war that was useless. I mean, I hadn't even heard of the Vietnamese before the Vietnam War.

Sometimes I am asked to explain 'the growing one-dimensionality of American society'. I'm not sure I understand. What one dimension does American life have, unless they mean that life is more materialistic in America?

---

[18] James Monroe, the 5th President of the United States

[19] Unclear who Quentin is referencing

That if you become rich, you've succeeded and you are right. I do think there's a certain materialism in American life that people are taught. The great thing is to "Get on!" Which is to say to earn more money than you earned last year, and that is what parents want for their children - but that's true of almost any set of people.

My parents wanted more money for me than I ever earned. Yet, though I was a freelancer from the age of about twenty-eight onwards, my mother would always say, "Are you still out of work?" You see, she wanted me to be in a secure job and I think nearly everyone wants that for their children. Americans perhaps want it more conspicuously, but I don't think that's bad.

America is, of course, a country guilty of conspicuous consumption. Americans waste a great deal. They like to feel that they will never come to the bottom of the barrel. "Have some more! Have plenty! Eat what you can!"

They are very hospitable and, I have found, very generous with everything they have. But that can, of course, be folly. The English are parsimonious. "You can have a little of it, not much. There isn't much." And that makes them very stingy and very thin-lipped. But, in truth, Britain is a small island with very little of anything.

American life is not divided into the haves and have-nots. It's divided into the people who are on television and the people who are not on television. Television is a quintessentially American thing. The movies are more influential on American life than anybody knows. Everybody wants to be a movie star because they want to be noticed. I once said the only point of fame is that it extends your social horizon, but a woman said, "That's not the only thing. You get a better table in a restaurant." I suppose that might be true, though goodness knows why you would want a better table in the first place. The food will still taste the same. But the point she was making was that she believed living with fame makes life one long party.

The American Dream is a very strange thing. It is principally concerned with happiness. Unfortunately, Americans mistake luxury for happiness, even though they are unconnected. You need plenty of money to be happy, but you don't need things. It's a lesson that seems harder for the young to understand. Middle-aged Americans don't want fast cars and large houses with swimming pools, but young people want them and think that they have a right to them. They will only be happy once they have them. In truth, I think the young will find themselves unhappier when they have all these things, because they will be devoid of excuses to begin looking inwardly at themselves.

Ideally, what you need is a lot of money and no possessions. Then you can be happy. I once saw a film called *Paris is Burning,* in which Ms. Livingston[20] asked one of the victims of Harlem what she really wanted. The answer was, "A house with a swimming pool and a large car." And while these words were being uttered, I thought to myself those are all burdens. With unlimited money and no possessions, you are free to go anywhere and do anything. Alternatively, I suppose you could be happy without money. You could just be content with your lot. I think most Americans would find that an unsatisfactory outcome however.

Of course, at my core I am British, although I try not to be too British. In truth, I've never learned American in spite of all of my observations. I once asked a man called

[20] Jennie Livingston, American director.

Arthur Cantor[21] whether I should learn the language before I came here, and he dismissed the idea by saying, "On no account! The more English you sound, the more likely you are to be believed." So, I speak English and I imagine that when Americans hear me they think to themselves, "He's pronouncing all of the words from beginning to end. He must really mean them."

I remember going to a wonderful meeting of American women, all of whom talked about beauty. A few days after I had left, I received a charming note from my hostess thanking me for having attended. It contained a strange sentence: "I've never conversed before with anyone who spoke in whole words." So, I don't know what Americans do. I know they speak whole sentences. Americans rarely use the full, original versions of words however, so perhaps this is what she meant. I mean, it would choke an American to say the word delicatessen. There are too many syllables. They would abbreviate it to 'deli' and instead spend the time they've saved shopping.

Up until this point, I hadn't really thought about the prevalence of abbreviated language in America. I think it's because everyone is trying to be cool. I don't think it's laziness. It's not as if they give up halfway through because the syntax is too elaborate. It's just unamerican to not use simplified conversation.

My principal experience of America is, of course, New York City. Previously, I have described my adopted home city as a twenty-four-hour, tax-deductible, Roman orgy. It pains me to say that's a slight exaggeration. But New York is full of people who want to know you, who want to speak with you, who want to take your photograph, and who

[21] Arthur Cantor, American theatrical producer.

want to record what you've said. It is for me anyway, and England was never like that. And while it might not be an orgy, it certainly feels like you are at a party. It is absolutely nonstop.

An Irishwoman once said to me, "The thing about New York is you can buy anything you want at any time of day. If you knew where to go, you could buy a secondhand bidet at four in the morning." I'm not sure why you would want to, but I wouldn't doubt that it's possible.

Here in New York, people are always inviting me out for lunch or dinner. When they do, I feel it is my duty to entertain them. I believe that's the only way to get a free meal, so that's what I do. It's become my job, more or less. I'm a professional luncher.

Back in England, I could never have lunch with anybody. People never invited me out to eat. They would worry what other people would think if they were seen out in public with me. The English are too snobbish and self-conscious. In America, people love to be stared at. And just in case they are not stared at sufficiently, they photograph you, which seems to always attract other people's attention.

These days I could never live anywhere else but here in America. Specifically New York City. In my opinion, you are freer in America than you are ever going to be anywhere else. You do as you please. You say what you like. You behave as you like. No one stops you until you actually shoot somebody. Then they stop you. Sometimes by shooting you as well. By contrast, in England you are not free to do anything.

The problem is that Americans don't want to live, they want to have lived. So, they are always being photographed with me to show the world that they have met me. It's very strange. In fact, one of the strangest compliments that I have received, I suppose you might even call it a gift, is that

I was recently made an Admiral of the Texas Navy. I received a letter to that effect and it read: "To all whom these presents shall some, greetings know ye that Quentin Crisp is hereby commissioned Admiral with the Texas Navy." I don't know who is to blame for that. I think it might be a joke. I mean Texas is protected by a navy, but it's the U.S. Navy rather than the state equivalent.

When I lived in England, I lived in London. To that end, I have always been a city rather than a country person. New Yorkers are much nicer than Londoners however because, as I have said before, New Yorkers are your friends. Londoners are nobody's friends. When the snow fell and then froze last winter, I couldn't walk a yard without fearing that I would fall down. Nevertheless I would venture out and a stranger, sometimes a young girl of about twelve, would come forward and take my arm and lead me across the difficult bits of the pavement. That would never happen in England. They would watch you through near-closed eyes waiting for you to fall so that they could laugh quietly at you.

I left England because I knew I could never be happy there. People are my only pastime, and in England people never, ever talk to you. So, I came to America and it is the single event that has most changed my life.

Ever since my mother took me to the movies as a boy, I feel I have always been American in my heart. Of course my mother wasn't happy about taking me to the movies. "The cinema," she would say, "is for servant girls! People with any taste go to the theatre." But eventually she would relent and take me. And when I began to gibber and twitch at the sight of New York on the screen, my mother would explain that what went on in real life was vastly different from what was portrayed in the films we saw. But she was wrong! Because every Londoner who goes to New York returns to say, "It's more like the movies than you'd ever dream!" And it is. They really do bring the dining room chairs out onto the pavement and sit there mopping their necks with Kleenex saying, "It isn't the heat. It's the humidity."

So, I knew that I wanted to see New York when I was young, but I never knew that I wanted to live here. It was only after I arrived, for the first time, and received such a warm welcome, that I knew I wanted to stay.

Los Angeles is quite different from New York City. There, everyone is either shooting a movie or stuck in their car in gridlock. There are no pedestrians. You can't walk up and down Wilshire Boulevard talking to people. By contrast in New York you can't wander up and down Second Avenue without speaking to any number of people.

Typically, people engage me rather than vice versa. I don't dare to speak to them, but they speak to me. And they typically tell me the story of their life while we're waiting for the traffic lights to change. No Englishman would ever do that.

I will never go back and live in London unless I am deported. I'm hopeful that will never happen, but it might because I do not yet have an American passport. I am not a naturalized citizen, you see, because I can't learn all of the things they test you on when you go for your citizenship test. My friends have more faith and tell me, "Well don't bother with any of that. Half of the people who come here even can't speak English."

That might be true, but a friend of mine once applied for U.S. citizenship and was asked three questions. I can't remember the first one, but he couldn't answer it. The second one was "What president succeeded Lincoln?" He didn't know that either. Then the third question was "How many Supreme Court judges are there?" And he also didn't know. So his inquisitor leaned forward and said to him, "You don't seem to be taking your situation seriously."

They clearly want you to know unto what you are swearing allegiance, which is natural enough. But it's hard for someone of my age. All the knowledge that I have, if indeed I have any, has been accumulated over the years. I'm not sure I'm even capable of learning new things. I am trying however.

Now, England has become a distant memory and I don't miss it at all. I don't think it misses me either. I only know a few people over there now: an Italian actress and a girl who was once the strongest girl in the world. They both write to me from time to time, but no one else that I can remember ever writes to me nor I to them. And that's natural enough.

There are no places in England I miss. I can't think of anything I did in England that I couldn't do here. You see, I lived a very simple life over there. I lived in Chelsea in a room much like my current room, except that it was larger and warmer and cheaper. But I accept my smaller accommodation here. All of this happiness has to be paid for, after all.

An Englishman once met me here and said, "You're the one who lives here permanently, aren't you?" And I said, "Yes." And he said, "Well, why?" And I said, "Because everywhere I go everybody talks to me." And he said, "I can't think of anything worse."

I just don't understand that point of view. I don't know why the English don't want strangers to talk to them. Of course, I am not likely thinking of something else at the time they approach me, so the conversation of a stranger never interrupts my train of thought. I also have no place to be, so I am never being delayed. I am therefore there to be spoken to, so it's a different existence from other people and one that I thoroughly enjoy.

Not everyone speaks to me. It's just a turn of phrase. I once said to a man that I went to meet faraway, "In Manhattan everybody speaks to you." And he said, "I told my mother you said everyone talks to you, and she said 'rubbish.'" And I said, "Well, of course, your mother is right. On the way here four people spoke to me. What about the four million that went by?" Yet, wherever I go in America, I have the feeling that I am welcome. In London, I never felt welcome.

To be fair, I generalize England too much. It is only southern England where nobody is your friend. In Yorkshire, people are at least matey. They're not really your friend, but at least they're matey. They say, "Good morning," to you when you meet them in the street and that's nice. It does give you the feeling that you're part of the world. But in London nobody ever speaks to you and I don't know why that is. They have a fear of their privacy being invaded, which is nonsense. What's the good of privacy unless it's invaded from time to time?

When I lived in London, I always felt different. I wanted to be spoken to. I wanted to be acknowledged. I wanted to be one with the world. Perhaps that was because I'm gay and I always felt separated? That's been my trouble. Had I been heterosexual, maybe I would have looked for someone to unite me with the world and then have children to further connect me with it. But, absent of a partner and children, I felt very detached from the world. I wanted to be acknowledged, but wasn't.

Wanting to be at one with the world set me apart from everyone else in London. Most British don't want to be at one with the world. They despise the world. I can't afford to despise anybody, so I am always glad to be at one with someone. The odd thing to me is that Americans say they like Britain and I wonder why?

These days, London is different from when I lived there. When I first appeared, swanning about London, I was not a beautiful young man, but I went on as though I were beautiful, which of course is half the battle. You assume that you are the center of attention and this creates the idea that you are the center of attention. It's self-fulfilling.

I returned to London last August[22] to promote a book called *Resident Alien.* I walked through Soho and there were chairs and tables on the pavement, which was very narrow, so you had to walk in the road in order to make your way past. That was never so in a time gone by. No one would have sat at a table outside, because of the weather, which was usually bad. But there they were, talking, eating, laughing, and waving to one another. Quite un-English! So, perhaps the people have changed since I lived there, even though the place looks much the same.

Now there is a snobbery in Soho, which I was surprised, even shocked, to see. When I went into certain pubs, where previously they wouldn't have even let me in, they welcomed me. Of course, what they were really welcoming was my fame, not me. Not the man, but the disguise. The persona.

Aesthetically, the pubs have all remained exactly the same. They were in the same location, decorated in the same way, with the same people drinking the same drinks in the same positions around the bar. Pub-goers aren't particularly keen on change. That's the appeal of a pub. It's always the same, which they find comforting.

While I was there I was asked if I missed anything

---

[22] 1998

about England. I answered truthfully by saying, "Only my gas fire." That annoyed people very much. But that's all I could think of. You see, in my current room in New York, or in any room in America in fact, there is no fireplace. So, in the winter the room is hot, because the whole house is heated like a greenhouse. In the summer it is cold because you want it to be as cool as possible. But in the twilight zone, about now, or in the autumn, you walk about the streets thinking, "This is wonderful. It's spring!"

Yet, when you get home you don't want to sit with your shoes and socks and your trousers and jacket on. You want to take everything off and lull about in a filthy dressing gown. And you can't because it isn't warm enough. And you can't make it any warmer. But, however poor you are in London, you have a little gas fire, and you think, "When we get home, we'll light the fire, and then we'll sit by it." Everyone in England has scorched shins and knees because they sit so near the fire.

The English, much like the Russians, love to suffer. Winston Churchill understood this perfectly and he played to it. He never told them that things would be wonderful, or that victory would be easy. He told the English they would suffer and they loved him for it. They rallied round him in order to suffer significantly, which is an English pastime. And he constantly made speeches saying that it would get worse and we must fight harder and give up more, but that we would eventually win the war against the Germans because the suffering would pay off. Having suffered so much in my personal life, I wasn't so keen that my burden be added to, but of course I had no say in the matter.

I was enamored when the American soldiers came, but then, after a while, I was ashamed of being English, because the English soldiers treated the American soldiers very badly. The English soldiers were envious, because they said their Americans counterparts had money to burn and could afford to give the girls such things as nylons and boxes of chocolates. I mean, they could. No wonder they were popular.

Of course, the real reason the American soldiers were a success was because they listened. The American soldiers would walk crabwise beside their dates so as to miss nothing. And girls like nothing more than feeling they are the center of attention.

An Englishman never listens to what his girlfriend says. My brother was never without a girl in tow and he would take her to a bar, sit her on a stool, and every twenty minutes he'd say to her, "Are you alright?" And she'd smile submissively toward him. Then he'd go on talking to his friends, and when she had gone, he would say to me, "What a boring woman." To which I would say, "What did you say to which she could make a witty reply?"

Englishmen never talk to women about subjects they might be interested in. So, of course, they are not a success. The girls have simply gotten used to it and now just talk to one another. But they might as well be single if they're just going to feel alone. I think they're just glad to be with a man of some kind and they put up with the lack of attention. It's sad, really.

During the war, I did not have a favorite American soldier. I knew several of them however. It was almost as if I knew them by braille, because we would meet in either the dark of the night or else in some dimly lit or blackened room. They used to think I was a woman in the dark.

I never had a favorite whom I claimed to be seeing or who rang me up. I just got to know a number of them, very briefly. They were very sweet. Some of the encounters were sexual. Some of them were just friendly, because Americans care much less about sex than the English.

There is a passage in the movie of *The Naked Civil Servant* when an American soldier addresses Mr. Hurt[23], and Mr. Hurt says, "You think I'm a woman, don't you?" And the man says, "I think so. Should I worry?" But what actually happened was a man spoke to me and I said, "You think I'm a woman, don't you?" And he said, "You waggle your fanny like a woman." And I said, "I should ignore that." And he said, "I'm trying to, but it's not so easy." Which is so much funnier. It's a pity that didn't get included in the film. I can't remember what I said back to that.

The English are so edgy about sex that they can't really be friends with anyone that they've had sex with, and they can't have sex with anyone that they're friends with. Americans don't care. They are just out to have a good time. And, of course, during the war the American soldiers were away from their local schoolteacher, clergymen, their employers and their parents, so anything went! They were much less guarded.

Life during the war was wonderful because, you see, first of all it was dark. And you could only go about by Braille, saying, "Wooden fence. We're not at the road yet. Ah, brick! Now we're at the end of the road." And you went on like that and you found your way to various places.

So, you were never conspicuous and you could go anywhere. You knew you were afraid because the only emotion that we know we feel is fear. And when the ground shook with antiaircraft fire and you could hear the shrapnel falling through the branches of the trees and tinkling on the pavement, you had to think that, if you

---

[23] John Hurt, English actor

stood still, you were no safer than if you walked on. So, you learned to disregard the war and that gave you the feeling that any moment might be your last. This was wonderful because then, like Mr. de la Mare[24], you looked your last on all things lovely every hour.

I never went hungry during the war. We ate in restaurants where there was always food. Very simple, but nice food, and plenty of it even though everything was rationed. We had coupons and I used to exchange my coupons. You had so many coupons for meat, and so many coupons for bread, and so many coupons for clothes, and so many coupons for sweets.

I always gave my ration of meat to someone who had a dog, because I could do without meat. In return she gave me her ration of sweets. I exchanged my tea coupons because I only drink one cup of tea a day and they gave me something else in exchange. There are some people in England who cannot live without tea, but I was not one of them. Some people drink it incessantly.

With all my sweet coupons I bought a lot of barley sugar, because that is said to be, to some extent, food and, to some extent, calming to the nerves. It all worked out alright. I don't ever remember going without anything. I remember people thinking we might all starve, but we never did.

When war broke out I bought, as I have said before, five pounds of henna. I should think that lasted about six months. I only put it on about every six weeks, because it was such trouble. But a little went a long way. And I did right to buy it because it became very scarce as it came from Egypt, which wasn't involved in the war but which

[24] Walter John de la Mare was a British poet

had difficulty in sending anything to England. When I ran out of henna I went to hairdressers to have my hair dyed, which I had never done before. Previously, I had always done it myself.

The war wasn't actually a bad time for me, though of course I never got bombed and the house in which I lived never fell down. In fact, no one I knew well ever got bombed. So, there was this atmosphere of terror in which we lived, but really we just got on living ordinary lives. Some people were terribly put out by the blackout, but I lived through it quite easily. Back then, homosexual sex was all about anonymity because of the shame and the illegality. So, you would meet someone and they would be careful not to tell you their name. That was the way I lived my life when I was young. I never asked anyone their name or where they lived or what they did, because they would have said, "Why do you want to know?" It was as if you would use the information against them somehow - blackmail them or the like. So, the natural darkness of the war years simply aided the anonymity of every encounter.

9. BILL, HILLARY AND MONICA

Let me start by saying that I think Monica Lewinsky is lucky to be alive. In the reign of Queen Elizabeth I, if anyone had caught sight of Elizabeth's sexual apparatus and afterwards bragged about it, he would have been instantly beheaded. Yet, hundreds of years later here in America, none of the women connected to President Clinton's infidelity have been beheaded. It's almost a shame. Not least of all for him.

The present state of affairs is very lenient in its treatment of the women involved. They are not censored at all, not even by public opinion, and I find that very strange. Of course, Linda Tripp was absolute hell. I mean, she persuaded someone who was her friend[25] to tell all and then recorded the conversation to use it against her. That's terrible. It's terrible because the harm done to friendship is worse than the harm done to morality.

Generally, Americans can distinguish between friendship and morality. However, though they can make the distinction, it seems to me they can't tell which is more

---

[25] Monica Lewinsky

important. They mostly think that morality is more important, but to me friendship is the only thing that really matters. We must maintain our friendships.

They once asked E.M. Forster[26] whether, if he had a friend whom he suspected was a spy, he would have had the courage to conceal the fact and he replied, "I hope I would." He regarded friendship as more important than his country. That may be going a bit too far, but I hope I would also defend such a person. Even if it meant potentially going to jail. I mean, if you knew that someone was stealing state secrets and you didn't report them, you could be complicit in treason.

Monica Lewinsky is probably just now realizing that she is never going to recover from this. When she is eighty, people will still remember her as the woman who behaved badly with the President of the United States. That to me is very sad because what occurred was a perfectly normal mistake, but the whole thing was amplified because of the historic setting.

The manner in which President Clinton was impeached to me said the right things about modern America. It said that sex does not matter. The only thing that matters was that he denied the offense. But, of course, that he was bound to do in order to preserve her reputation. To me it was a noble thing that he did and not a sin. I don't even regard it as a political sin.

I still think Clinton is a wonderful man, especially since he has gone on as though nothing unpleasant happened. I think both he and his wife have dealt with this situation quite wonderfully. They have gone on in spite of everything and in the end they have triumphed. I respect them as a

[26] Edward Morgan Forster was an English novelist

unit, as a married couple. Even though you are aware of my thoughts regarding marriage.

Mrs. Clinton in her own right is quite wonderful because if you are a president's wife they are going to give you hell no matter what you do. No matter what you say. No matter what you wear. If you take no notice of what your husband does and you decorate the White House, people will say, "You're frivolous." But if instead you take a great interest in your husband's work people say, "You're trying to take over the country." So, you can never get it right. Instead, Mrs. Clinton has steered a middle course, one that has left her practically unscathed. I would very much like to see her run for senator. I don't know why some people object, but her critics have said some pretty horrible things on that front. In the end I think the criticism she receives is principally because she's a woman. American men think that politics should be an exclusively male pursuit.

England would, of course, be suitably shocked by the Lewinsky-Clinton situation, because sex is shocking in England. Sex over there is a sin. But in France it would make no difference. When Mr. Mitterrand[27] died, his mistress walked on one side of the coffin and his wife on the other. Nobody took any notice of this because it is understood in France that married men have to have some kind of outlet for their energy other than their wives.

I remember being in Minneapolis and hearing people say terrible things about Mr. Clinton. They said, "What about his marriage vows?" Well, what about them? His marriage vows were made years ago. If I had to abide by the decisions and promises I made when I was twenty-two,

[27] François Mitterrand served as President of France from 1981 to 1995

I should be in a terrible mess. So, I don't think they're valid past a certain period of time. I don't think anyone really takes their marriage values seriously after the first twenty-five years.

Marriage vows, like marriage, are a mistake of course, but men make them to be with a woman who wants children. The vows ensure the children she bears are yours and in return you offer to keep them, look after them and pay for them. That was what preoccupied people in times gone by. When men went to war they left their wives in chastity belts. They didn't want to have to look after a brood of bastards when they returned.

Of course, everything about Mr. Clinton's impeachment is on television. It's must-see viewing because he's the President. I suppose the public has the right to know what is going on and to decide whether he is the right person to hold their destiny in his hands, but to my mind broadcasters need to be careful how they present it to their audiences. It shouldn't be entertainment. They shouldn't make it shocking, salacious or nasty in any way, if they can possibly avoid it.

One of the worst things that has happened to modern life is the press, both the television and the print media. They will say anything. And there is a law in America that says that, if you have placed yourself in the public domain, you cannot sue anybody for libel, which accounts for why that horrid Kitty Kelly can write those terrible books about Ms. Taylor[28]. In England it is altogether different. There you can sue people much more easily and all you have to prove is that the libel is malicious.

Oddly, however, the business of suing people is a much

[28] Elizabeth Taylor, British-American actress

bigger industry and pastime in America. Here, everyone sues everyone and they expect rich rewards. Or their lawyers do. You see, if you can make two million dollars on a libel case, or a case of any kind, half of it goes to the lawyers and the other half has to be split with the IRS. I suppose you still end up with something - damages they call it - and therefore the temptation is there to start trouble or seek revenge.

Mr. Clinton's style is, I think, satisfactory. He is very unemphatic. He doesn't wear peculiar clothes or have a peculiar haircut or do anything that would make a person dislike him on sight. He looks like a businessman, and that's a good thing because he is in business. He is in the business of ruling the country. His method of speaking is never too colloquial and never too highbrow. He has made himself into the average man, and not many politicians have ever succeeded at that.

Few politicians can maintain a style. Moreover, many don't even have one. They make grand speeches containing innumerous promises, which they can't possibly keep. They make political gestures that have no meaning. I don't think Mr. Clinton has ever said anything, except in the case of Monica Lewinsky, that he has subsequently had to deny. To me that's a good thing. I think he's one of our best Presidents. Of course, he has to curb his sexual appetite, or at least exercise it with more discretion. But it is very difficult for a public figure to conduct a private life anyway. Most public figures find it is impossible. And if you are going to try and have a private life, you have to work very hard to make sure it doesn't leak out. Inevitably it always does and inevitably it always causes a scandal. But the fault is ours, not theirs. We don't want our leaders to be real people. We don't want them to be fallible like us, but they came from us so how can they not be. Then we become fixated on the details and hold it against them.

10. THE BRITISH ROYAL FAMILY

Every fourth of July, America celebrates the casting off of its colonial rulers and the establishment of the country that I now call home. That historic American attitude towards the British royal family was short-lived however. At independence they considered them tyrants. Now they are given the movie-star treatment. Of course, Americans can do that because they don't have to live with them day-in and day-out.

In spite of their modern-day fairytale-inspired enthusiasm for the British royals, replicating them here would be a bad idea. Moreover, I think America is fine the way it is. Monarchy-free. England exists because of royalty and royalty exists in England because the English believe in privilege. In America there is no privilege. If you work at it, you can become President. Well, not, I think, if you are black, for as I have said before, America will never recover fully from slavery. Royal privilege is altogether different.

You see, you don't have to do anything to become King of England. It's all bloodline. Monarchy would never work here. People would be too angry. They would say, "Why is the Queen so rich? She doesn't do a stroke of work!"

In truth, of course, nothing could be further from the truth. The Queen works almost every day on behalf of the government and country and, I would guess, her life is very tiring and above all very lonely. I would never want to be Queen of England. I wouldn't even want to be Prime Minister.

In spite of what I have said about England over the years, England is more broadminded than people imagine. We have had a woman prime minister in the form of Mrs. Thatcher[29] and, a long time ago, a Jewish prime minister by the name of Mr. Disraeli[30]. In America, the furthest they've veered away from the White-Anglo-Saxon-Protestant model has been an Irish-American president. But you could never have a Jewish president or a black president or a woman president.

The Queen, of course, was not our first female national leader either. Not that the Queen really rules England; her role is more advisory. It is the prime minister who rules England. But before the current queen we had Queen Elizabeth I and Queen Victoria.

Victoria was only twenty-three when she became the Queen of England and she reigned for almost sixty years. She must have married Prince Albert fairly young because she had any number of children. Prince Albert was not favored because he had a German accent, although so had Queen Victoria, but he spared her several mistakes. Without him, she would have written to foreign princes saying how angry she was at some trivial insult. He would calm her down saying, "Oh, I don't think I would send that." And she didn't.

---

[29] Margaret Thatcher, first female British Prime Minister

[30] Benjamin Disraeli, former British Prime Minister

Queen Victoria also had a great sense of duty. She married off all of her daughters to German princes in the hope that it would prevent World War I. Of course it didn't. But the idea was good in theory. Nothing cements an alliance in Europe better than a royal wedding. Well, providing it is the right kind of wedding.

When King Edward VIII wanted to marry the twice-divorced Wallis Simpson it caused a constitutional crisis. It was the biggest story of its day in England and totally preoccupied the masses. When you went into a shop to buy half a pound of potatoes, before the shopkeeper said, "What would you like?" he said, "What do you think she said today?" It was Mrs. Simpson, whom everyone was either for or against. Most were chiefly against. But I regard Mrs. Simpson as the first American martyr, because Edward had already told his father, George V, that he would never ascend to the throne. He told him this in the presence of a man called Fruity Metcalfe. It's hard to believe, these days. I mean, the name is so ludicrously English that you start to laugh.

Fruity Metcalfe, whose real name was Edward Dudley Metcalfe, was known to the editor of *Vogue*, Diana Vreeland. Ms. Vreeland knew Fruity Metcalfe, and Fruity Metcalfe told her that he had been with Edward VIII when he had told his father of his intention never to become king. So, really, the establishment used Mrs. Simpson as an excuse to force his abdication and avoid a hollow reign because his fate had already been predetermined.

People were very unkind towards Mrs. Simpson, saying that she wanted to be the Queen of England. She didn't want anything of the sort. All she wanted was to be herself. And she had style. Mrs. Simpson said, "No one can ever be too rich or too thin." She wasn't a good-looking woman, but at least she was thin. And she made that straight-up-

and-down, that very severe quality, into her style. Edward, of course, was just a drip. I mean, he fell into her hands. He did exactly as she said and, once they were together, he never made a decision again, which is what he wanted. He wanted a wife to take over.

Then his brother, George VI, ascended to the throne and he was entirely unsuited to being king. He had never been groomed to be monarch, whereas his brother - as the heir apparent - had. George VI stuttered for a start and had to learn how not to stutter.

The only person to benefit from the Simpson scandal was the Queen Mother, because she was the wife of George VI. She had a wonderful time and was Queen of England by default! She dealt with that by loving everybody, and that is really the function of a monarch. You must say, "However stern I am and however much I cost you, I love you all." It's very difficult to do because you will never please everybody. You will never win over everyone. They will say, "Why have you got all that money? You never do any work." Whereas that is just the appearance of the royal family. Most work like mad every day, opening hospitals, schools, bridges and buildings. Being the patron of various charities. Attending public functions. And they have to always be on their best behavior, smiling and nodding.

The current Queen doesn't have the capacity to say that she loves us, however. I can't imagine Queen Elizabeth II saying that ever. It's odd that she didn't inherit that from her mother. I think only the Queen Mother can or would say such a thing.

You see, the Queen Mother, who received that title when her husband died and her daughter became monarch, is now in a wonderful position because she is the grandmother of the nation. And there is always a more pleasant relationship between a grandmother and her grandchildren than between a mother and her children. A mother has to deal with the children. The grandmother regards the children as toys. She gives them sweets, which make them sick, and she says, "Don't tell your mother that I gave you this." And it's great fun for her and for the grandchild because they're not being watched, they're not being criticized.

After I was praised for my role playing Queen Elizabeth I in *Orlando*, I have often been asked if I have any plans to play Queen Elizabeth II. It's as if, in some people's minds, one follows from the other. Like they are a pair or a boxed set. I have no plans to play Queen Elizabeth II, but I am terribly sorry for her because everyone around her has behaved so badly.

I think most people feel pity and empathy for the Queen. Why did Princess Margaret have to divorce Mr. Armstrong-Jones[31]? They lived in Kensington Palace where they would have had a job meeting, let alone fighting. Why did Princess Anne have to divorce her husband? Everyone was divorcing everyone and behaving as badly as they could. And Princess Diana, about whom my opinions are known, she behaved worst of all. But the Queen remained unshaken and that is all she could do. She said, "It is a question of training. I hope I have been well trained." It's a sad state of affairs. I think she must be very lonely.

You see in England adultery is condoned, but divorce is not. Adultery can be conducted in secret, whereas divorce is a public act. In America, the opposite is true. Divorce is almost worshipped. Every American woman knows that marriage is for a little while, but that alimony is

[31] Antony Charles Robert Armstrong-Jones, 1st Earl of Snowdon

forever.

In England, kings have never behaved well. King William IV had ten illegitimate children. His wife, Queen Adelaide, would never have divorced him. Edward VII behaved so outrageously with his little friends that the English public knew their names: Mrs. Langtry, Ms. Beneni, Mrs. Bernhardt, Mrs. Keyser and Mrs. Keppel. But Queen Alexandra would never have divorced him. And when he lay dying, she said, "Let Mrs. Keppel be sent for." Now isn't that wonderful? She was his wife, the Queen of England, but she knew that at that moment she did not matter. And Queen Alexandra was just as beautiful as Princess Diana.

I think Diana tried to bring down the royal family, which was a great pity because it was not up to her to do that. I don't know why she became a saint because she seemed to be so self-indulgent. And they say, "Well, she was only a girl." I mean, at the end of her life she had children old enough to go to school. She was a middle-aged woman complaining about not being loved? I mean, it's absolute rubbish. Princess Diana thought she mattered. What gave her that idea? And she could have learned to be the Queen of England if she'd stayed with it, but she mucked it up. She was more concerned with gallivanting and jet-setting.

Oddly, the subject of who will succeed Queen Elizabeth II is one that people seem keen to discuss. There is no discussion to be had, however. Prince Charles is her heir and that's all there is to it. The rules cannot be rewritten to make someone else king. That would be treason.

I do think that when Charles is declared king, however, he will probably rule for only a little while before abdicating in favor of his eldest son, who is untouched by scandal or the dislike of the people. The British monarchy will go on, and it should go on. I think the monarchy is a good thing. You see, the divine right of kings has ceased to exist, but it still exists in the minds of English people. It would be like denying a lottery-winner their jackpot. They were just born into a fortunate position, or unfortunate if you regard the shackles of royalty as being more of a burden than a blessing.

The Queen, of course, is very rich, but the wealth isn't really hers. It belongs to the country. She is just the custodian. She couldn't wake up one day and decide to sell a palace. There would be outrage. It is interesting how her entourage are trying to make her look more like a real person, however. I think this is the principal reason she always carries a handbag with her. We know it's not full of money, because we are told the royals don't carry money. Queen Mary, of course, carried nothing. And if she wanted to buy anything, one of her ladies-in-waiting would come forward and pay for it. And that made her look very regal to me. I like the song and dance of royalty. I like all of the pomp.

England is one of the last places in the world where there is a great deal of ceremony. Who else wears a crown anymore? Who else travels to parliament in a horse-drawn coach and sits there in ermine, clutching all of the gold regalia, to read a speech?

The people that meet her still have to walk backwards before her. This is because it is considered disrespectful to show her your back. But if all that protocol and history were abandoned, what would be left? Simply a woman who has inherited a position where she has no real power and no ability to express what she actually believes. I mean, she doesn't make laws. Her ancestors used to, but they soon wised up to the fact that absolute power means you are the only person to blame when things go wrong.

Nevertheless, the monarchy is not an outdated institution for England, because the English still believe in privilege. In England everyone knows their place. And everyone accepts that they cannot improve their place by working. It's the exact opposite of America. In England, people who emerge from one class into another are despised. They are the rule-breakers. They are considered *nouveau riche* rather than rich. The French expression is used to make it more stylish, which is absurd, of course.

One of the underappreciated benefits of the class system, however, is that everyone can stay where they are and complain about it. Complaining, like queuing, is a very English thing. In America, no one stays where he is. If he doesn't like his situation, he changes it. He works hard, and he is praised because he has worked and gone from being a gardener to being a landowner. That's what marks the difference between England and America. Anyone can be president, but no one else can be the Queen of England.

Of course, the downside to the limitless upward mobility that exists in America is that, if you haven't made it, you have no one to blame but yourself. It must be a terrible burden and one that the working classes of England will never be concerned with. It sounds absurd, of course, but it takes a lot of weight off people's shoulders, I assure you.

11. AUSTRALIANS

I went to Australia in 1978 during what they call their winter. Whilst I was there they lamented, "Oh. You came during winter." I said, "Don't apologize. An Australian winter is better than an English summer."

There were flowers the size of table mats on the trees in Australia in winter. The air there is like diamonds. They lack nothing. I tried to discourage them from being a nation of 'Madame Butterflies', because they stand on the coast and wait for the wisp of smoke on the far horizon. They think it's all out there, but I told them, "It's all in here. You've got it all. You have the weirdest animals, but you can ignore them."

The Australians make wonderful films and write wonderful novels. The film called *Picnic at Hanging Rock* is a frightening movie, but it's wonderful nevertheless. *The Adventures of Priscilla, Queen of the Desert* is a delightful and wounding movie. It's infinitely better than the feeble film *To Wong Foo, Thanks for Everything! Julie Newmar*, which was disneyfied and dismal. But *Priscilla* was raw, moving and incredibly real.

Australians are more like Americans than they are like English people. They love England, but they hate the

English. In a way, it's similar to the way the English view the French and France. When I asked Australians what they liked about England, I never got a reply. But I decided that it was the littleness of England that appealed to them.

Australia is so vast a country, though sparsely populated, that I consider its relationship with England to be like that between King Kong and Ann Darrow. I remember taking a companion to see the 1933 film, starring Ms. Wray[32] as Ann Darrow, and at that very dramatic moment when Ms. Ray lays gibbering across King Kong's wrist, my friend, in a voice shrill with irritation, said, "I can't think what he sees in her!" I suggested that what he saw in her was her littleness. Her fragility.

I loved Australia. I saw all the great cities of its world except Darwin, which had been blown down a couple of years before on Christmas Day. A typhoon, as Mr. Conrad[33] calls it, came down from off the coast of Japan. Previously, they had never caught the Northern-Western coast of Australia, but on Christmas Day in 1974 'Cyclone Tracy' hit Darwin.

The Australians had never known a typhoon, and they went and hid in their cellars. When the typhoon passed, they came out and everything was calm. Then the typhoon came back and took the tops off all the houses! Darwin lost its nerve. Now it's a city devoted to business and commerce, but no one will ever live there again. It's a big town, the capital of the Northern Territory.

I don't think I want to live in Australia. They're a maritime people. Everyone has his boat and stores it in Sydney, which has a harbor so enclosed that when Captain

---

[32] Vina Fay Wray, Canadian-American actress

[33] Joseph Conrad, Polish-British author

Cook sailed nearby, he didn't recognize that it was a harbor and went straight past.

And now there's a bridge, perhaps the longest bridge in the world, across the harbor. And in the harbor are all the private boats of all the Australians. And they love to drink beer and sail their boats. That is their pastime. I think Australians resent the fact that England still regards them as a colony. They want to be free of that. One day, a Ghandi-style Australian will arise and protest, and England will give up Australia, and it'll be a free country. Then there will be no more Queensland - how can there be without a Queen?

Australia is vast. While I was there, I went from, I should think, Melbourne to Perth, over territory which gives you an impression there's a road going from Melbourne to Perth. And it looks as though they could see Perth when they began to make the road - which would be impossible - because it's absolutely straight. And halfway across there's a turning to the right, which goes to Alice Springs, which is in the center of Australia.

If your car broke down on the road from wherever you are to Perth, there would be nothing for you to do but to get out of the car, lie on the ground in the shadow of the car, and move when the shadow moved and wait. Because if you said, "I will go inland and see if I can get help," there is nothing. There are no hedges, no pubs, no roads, no lakes, no rivers, no anything. There is just desolation.

They once tried to counter the desolation with The Snowy River Project, which was a disaster. The Snowy River Mountains are in the south-east and someone said, "If we bomb the Snowy River, it will flow back into the interior and irrigate the land." And they did just that, but the flow of the redirected river was simply absorbed by the desert.

The other commonality between Australia and America is the similarity that exists between Australian Aborigines and Native Americans. I saw a number of Aborigines sitting outside of town halls while I was there. They looked forlorn and absolutely desperate. They have nothing. It has all been taken away from them, much like Native Americans. But I liked Australia a lot.

12. PHILOSOPHERS AND HUMAN BEINGS

Why is there something rather than nothing? I don't know why. When I was at school, I was once on a bridge looking down into some water and, for a moment, the boy I was with and I imagined that we were looking down into the sky. I turned to him and said, "Supposing it were all sky?"

"But why sky?" he replied.

And for a moment, I thought. "That's right. There could be nothing. Not even space! I don't know why it's there, I can't explain it."

The boy felt frightened when he realized he was nothing. I too felt quite strange. I remember thinking, why? Why anything? And the whole world disappeared. And that was my first existential experience, I suppose.

You see, the universe has no meaning and there was no purpose in my being born into it. I never listen to conversations which begin, "We are all put into the world for…" because we weren't put into the world. We just happened and we have no purpose and that's fine.

Why such obvious statements seem to annoy other people, I don't know. I was once talking in this way to a middle-aged housewife at a painting class in the suburbs and she said, "Even though life may have no meaning, I still don't understand those people who take their own lives. Life may have no meaning, but it's still very nice living it."

Her comment surprised me and I thought, I agree. Life doesn't have to have a purpose. It's still alright and for most people a lot better than the alternative.

I suppose if your life has been hard, you've never had what you want, never had enough to eat and never had anywhere to live, you think, "Why am I here?" That must be terrible and frightening for most people. It's no wonder the poor turn to religion. It gives them both hope and purpose.

I don't think I have any purpose however. I could give myself a purpose, if I like. I could say I am here to change the world, to make people better, but I really don't believe that. I don't feel driven to do anything. I simply live my life from day to day and I enjoy it. Most importantly, I can enjoy it without taking anything from other people that they don't want to give. That to me is very important.

To suggest we're put on this earth with a purpose suggests that we have been put here by some force greater and wiser than ourselves. I don't think that is true. I think we are entirely accidental, and once we have come to terms with that we just have to get through it somehow.

Tabula rasa is a Latin phrase that is typically translated as 'blank slate'. As a concept, it means we start out with nothing. Wordsworth[34], of course, did not believe that we start out with nothing. He said: "Our birth is but a sleep and a forgetting; The Soul that rises with us, our life's Star, Hath had elsewhere its setting And cometh from afar; Not in entire forgetfulness, And not in utter nakedness, But

[34] William Wordsworth, English Romantic poet

trailing clouds of glory do we come From God, who is our home: Heaven lies about us in our infancy!"

In other words, he thought we brought with us some supernatural feeling at the very least, if not evidence of the purpose of life. But I don't think life has any purpose. Instead, I think we just fill in the time between the cradle and the grave.

The Earth is but one of an infinite number of planets. The notion that we are special is ludicrous. We are accidental, even though we were lucky enough to beat the odds to obtain life in the first place. On a related matter, I was once asked by a young gentleman, during my one-man show, if I believed in extraterrestrial life and I told him that I did. As I resident alien, how could I have said otherwise? But in truth, I can't say that I do believe there is life out there.

At another show I was asked by a lady what it means to be human. Having been asked this question, I was immediately sorry that I was not a scholar and had no philosophical point of view to express. More than that, since I do not regard myself as a real human being I find myself doubly unqualified to answer the question.

Biologically, I am human. I know that. But what I have in common with the rest of the human race seems to end there. I lack the urgency and purpose that others seem to have. My sister reminded me, before she died, that she and my mother used to sit on either side of the fireplace in our family home, occupying themselves with knitting or else writing letters on their laps. I was a child, and merely lay on the rug between the two of them. Once an hour one of them would say, "Why don't you get something to do?"

And I would say, "Why should I?"

This remains a question I cannot answer. Why should I have something to do?

There is, of course, the theory that time is money and, as I have said elsewhere, I like money, though only to save it, never to spend it. It is an American theory, but its application means that while I am doing nothing I am not earning money, which is sad. But if I were rich, I would never do anything. I was once asked by a newspaper journalist, "If you suddenly had a million dollars, what would you do?" And I said, "Go to bed, and never get up again." This was a great disappointment to the writer who posed the question, but idleness is my only occupation and people are my only hobby.

If I regard what makes a thing human, and perhaps I was asked precisely because I am not a human being and therefore have a detached view of the subject, I would say it was a preoccupation with the idea of death. The reason why people do not live alone and do not spend hours doing nothing is because they can hear the time ticking by.

Those who are not hopeless are worried that one day their life will end. But, if you live long enough, of course, you long for it to end. That's been my desire in recent times. I only hope to become extinct. But before all that, you must try everything: have children, behave in such a way that monuments are built to you, rule the world, have streets and theaters named after you, and write your autobiography. These are ways to stay alive and this seems to be a preoccupation among human beings.

If being human has any other special aspect it is that in every human being there are two people. One who does and one who sits in judgment on the other. The doing person acts irresponsibly, or nobly, or wisely, or foolishly, according to the mood or the situation. But inside him, further away, is an abstract spiritual being who never changes and who sits in judgment on him.

This situation becomes evident when we hear people

say, "I was ashamed of myself." Who is ashamed of whom? It is this duality between the active living organism and the contemplative inner-self that sits in judgment that constitutes the whole human being. Upon greater reflection this is, I think, what constitutes a human being.

13. MARRIED COUPLES

When I was a young man, a great many married women told me their troubles. This led me to ask these unhappy creatures why they got married in the first place. They invariably told me: "I got married to get away from my mother and father." If I inquired why, having flown the nest and found themselves in merely a different form of entrapment, they did not now leave their spouses, they would ask of me, "Where would I go?"

Many long, dark years later, when a niece of mine, with no particular victim in mind, prophesized that she would one day marry, I couldn't refrain from uttering an incredulous exclamation, "Why would you get married?" Her response was, "Everybody does." Hers was a less tragic excuse, but hardly more sensible.

These days neither of these answers is still relevant. A girl can leave home merely in search of adventure, and marriage is no longer a state into which every woman scrambles by any means whatsoever. This only makes it harder to understand why anyone at all enters into matrimony, least of all people who have flouted every other convention.

I think it is all the fault of mothers. Even now, with

George Bush's[35] family values depreciating at an alarming rate, most people's mothers are married. We can therefore safely assume that they have had rotten lives and all they want for their daughters are lives that are equally rotten. It's only logical. Their sons they leave alone. They have already, reluctantly, learned from their husbands that men marry only when all is lost, when it is certain that the girl with eyes the size of saucers and red hair down to her waist will never arrive.

Daughters are another matter. They are fair game. As such, mothers constantly threaten with such remarks as, "If you go around looking like that, you'll end up alone." I know that in polite families answering back is forbidden, but the only logical response to such admonitions is, "Yes, and thank God for that!"

Luckily, the future is not as black as it might seem. The disastrous chain of events I have described will soon be broken. In the near future, everyone will be born in a little glass dish and will be looked after by a gentleman wearing rimless spectacles and a white coat, who not only utters no threats but who also never says, "And after all I've done for you…"

No one can have happiness and marriage. Anyone who wants happiness must pursue it for its own sake. A woman must choose and, if she opts for matrimony, then forever after, however miserable she becomes, she must say to herself, "Well, I'm married."

When American newspapers first displayed photographs of Princess Diana above such captions as, "Is she happy?" I tried to explain that this was not the point. But I reckoned without the difference between the

[35] George H. W. Bush, 41st President of the United States

temperaments of England and America. In England, happiness has a bad name. There, the pursuit of happiness - which every American considers to be his right - is deemed to be a frivolous objective. The British do not want to be happy: they want to be right.

Furthermore, royal marriages are political alliances, not personal unions. When Princess Mary's[36] fiancé unexpectedly died, she simply married the next brother in line for the English throne. All that is required of a royal couple is to produce enough sons to secure the succession and to stand smiling beside one another at public ceremonies. After all, if they live in Buckingham Palace, they don't have to see terribly much of each other anyway.

The problem is altogether greater for married couples in England who live in humbler circumstances. I ask some of them how they manage to remain wise, witty, kind and beautiful for twenty-four hours a day. They giggle, but they don't tell me, and yet this is the pertinent question. If a wife were ever to utter the words, "Oh, do shut up," her marriage would be over. The phrase must surely run through her mind endlessly. But there it has to stay unless she wants to enter a convent. At least, that's how it used to be.

At ninety, I feel that the only thing that has changed in society is, of course, that marriage is admitted to be a failure. I recently saw a film in which a man said to a woman, "If you wanted monogamy, why didn't you marry a swan?" His point, of course, is that men are not suited to monogamy and this is perfectly obvious. Women go on as though men have only a certain number of erections in a lifetime, and if they wasted them on some other woman the

[36] Mary of Teck

wife would somehow be missing out.

In reality, you can't expect anyone to love you only, unless you consider yourself to be the wisest, wittiest, kindest, most beautiful, and wealthiest woman in the world. Women are full of delusions, but I can't see that any of them believe that. So, what are they crying about? He found someone, temporarily or otherwise, that he likes better. It doesn't mean he doesn't like you. It's just that he's used to you. You're no longer exotic. You're no longer untamed.

It's because of the vow of marriage that a woman feels she has exclusive rights over her husband. Why make a vow of marriage? Why say you'll stick to one person only, when you really have no idea what else is out there. You're not making an informed choice. I mean, people marry in their twenties and end up living to be seventy. That's fifty years during which you're stuck with the same person. It's a terrible penance physically, emotionally, intellectually and sexually. How bored must they get? How boring must they be?

By taking a vow of marriage, you make a useless self-sacrifice. You're making a public gesture of throwing your life away. I saw a film the other day in which a woman seized the lapels of a man's coat and said, "Do you really love me?" And he replied, "If I say yes, what does it mean?" What does it mean? How do you prove that you love someone? Even to yourself. In reality, when you get to the end of your life, if they are still there, you only know that they didn't find anyone better. It doesn't mean to say they weren't looking. It doesn't even mean that you were the love of their life. You just happened to spend the most time with them.

So, marriage is a dead loss. It's a mistake. I suspect it

was invented by the troubadours[37]. They would find a fair lady to whom they had never spoken. She leaned out of a tower window and waved her scarf. And they fought battles in which the issue was of no account to them. They did it for her sake. Why? Who the hell is she? It's absolute nonsense. It's all a delusion. And now, of course, that is over, but the vestiges of it remain.

It's tragic to observe how husbands and wives interact. There are some men who will say to their wives, "What are you looking at? Why are you looking over there?" And the wife is just looking around, not necessarily with intent. But they will argue, which is nonsensical, because by being jealous he is paying her a compliment. Of course, some women get wise to this. There used to be women who deliberately created situations in which they were seen with other people by their husbands, and tried to give the appearance that an affair was either pending or actually happening. I think that's playing with fire. Deliberately provoking jealousy seems like a great idea up until the point when the husband flies into an ungovernable rage.

While I'm on the subject, I'm always dumbfounded why people confuse jealousy and envy. Men will say, "He doesn't like me because of the job I've got. He's jealous." In truth they are envious. Envy is a preoccupation with what you haven't got and wish you had. Jealousy is a desire to keep what you have.

The way to deal with jealousy, if it's becoming problematic, is by calming it. By reassuring the jealous party that you are theirs or that there is no danger of you being whisked away by someone else. Even if that's what you secretly want.

---

[37] Troubadours were poets during the Middle Ages

Back to marriage. At the end of the day, marriage consumes an individual like fire. Married couples are individuals who have surrendered their own identities and dreams in return for fulfilling a preordained destiny that in reality was, at best, missold and, at worst, a fraud.

The truest love is self-love. And it is the only love that you can know with certainty is reciprocated.

14. DRAG QUEENS AND PERFORMERS

Though the saying goes 'imitation is the sincerest form of flattery', I think it's important to note that flattery is very different from giving a compliment. Flattery is superficial. A true compliment is heartfelt.

Anyway, no one's ever tried to be like me, I'm happy to say, so I've never been flattered in that way. And since I think you should have a style which precludes imitation, my lack of imitators could mean that I've been successful in this effort.

The stars of the past were, I think, encouraged to foster their idiosyncrasies to become more like themselves. And, of course, the imitators settled on them because they became so easy to imitate. Mae West and Bette Davis being just two examples. Nowadays you have actresses who cannot be imitated because they're so different from film to film. They are actually allowed to act, which is probably a win for entertainment.

However I don't think people should assume that you are making fun of somebody just because you are imitating them. That seems to me very sad and quite mistaken. People imitate others because they like them. It would take a very strange individual to imitate someone they didn't like, because surely they would hate themselves all the time they were doing it.

I do think imitators can be bitchy however, and I don't think that's alright. I don't think you should imitate people so as to exaggerate their mannerisms into absurdity, but then I don't approve of bitchiness of any kind, so why should I approve of that?

I don't think I've ever been bitchy. I've tried not to be. I can't say I haven't been, but since I despise it in other people, I've tried my best to expunge it from my own actions. Bitchiness is merely to make a joke at someone else's expense, and of course the only people who laugh at those are whomever isn't offended.

Charles Pierce[38] was an imitator and I liked him because he always acknowledged me if I was in the audience. He imitated various people but he was stuck with the people of his own generation. He imitated Tallulah Bankhead, but now no one can remember who Tallulah Bankhead was. That put him in a very difficult position, but I liked his shows.

And I do love Joey Arias[39]. Joey Arias is everywhere! Whenever I go to a place, he's always there. And when he came to interview me for a film made by a German director, he came disguised as himself and he looked so different that I wouldn't have known him had he not introduced himself to me. He was a nice-looking, blond young man, with a white face, a mulberry-colored mouth and a black wig. All that added on to make him a mask. Not merely made-up, but an actual mask, almost. And why he does that, I don't know, but I should think it's grown on

---

[38] Charles Pierce, American female impersonator

[39] Joey Arias, American performance and drag artist

him. At first, he was just made up, and then he was more made-up, and then he was made-up so much that he was Joey Arias. He's wonderful.

I don't think Mr. Arias could portray me in a movie however, but he could if he appeared as himself. The thing is, I've never done drag. I've only once worn women's clothes and that wasn't in order to appear as a drag queen, it was to appear as a woman, which is different. When you want to wear drag, you want to make fun of women. I wanted to be a woman, which is altogether different.

Boy George[40] is something of an imitator. I admire Boy George because he was only about twenty-two when he was asked all the difficult questions. He was asked whether he preferred the company of men or women, and he said, "I like to be with the people who like to be with me." That, of course, is what most people feel. I can't imagine anyone looking at their life and saying, "I don't know enough women. I must find some acceptable women." Instead you end up knowing the people who turn up and never leave. Hopefully because they like spending time with you.

When I worked for him, Mr. George was fine. He arrived with his merry men in the apartment where I was to speak certain words at the beginning of one of his records. He had written them out large so that I could sit there and read them. And he was very business-like. He came, he told me what to do, and he left. He knows just what he wants. And Boy George has a style that's so uniquely his, like my own is to me.

There is a man named Mr. Bloolips, who is also called Mr. Bourne[41], and he is going to play the part of me in

---

[40] Boy George, British singer, songwriter, DJ and fashion designer

[41] Peter Bourne, British actor, drag queen and activist

some show in England. He's going to do a performance in which he imitates me. I think his imitation of me is the whole show. It's to be done in Shepherd's Bush, which is a terrible outpost of London, near Hammersmith. Whether people will go, I shall hear later, but I have no idea what it's like. He will probably send me what the press has said about him. He's very nice. Mr. Bourne teaches at the Old Vic School. That his students take him seriously surprises me, because they must know he takes his camp act all over the world.

Speaking of which, I should talk about my experience on gay cruises, which is not to be confused with gay cruising. I have been on four such cruises, in fact, and they were all very nice.

When I boarded my first I had to wonder if all of the ship's crew had been told in advance what kind of cruise it was. I mention this because there are only three types of worker aboard a cruise ship: there are the people who make the ship go, whom you never see and who are all oriental; there are those who tidy up the cabins and serve the meals, who are all typically black; and then there's a 'show' crew of people who wander about the deck dressed in enamel-like uniforms covered with as much gold braid as one can safely stitch onto a single garment. The latter group stand around grandly and occasionally look out to sea and make pronouncements. They don't actually do a thing. They are always Greek.

On each of my cruises, the ship's guests have all been exclusively gay Americans. I suppose I was notionally part of the entertainment. On one of the cruises, Wayland Flowers and Madame were also part of the entertainment troop. I didn't get to see his act, unfortunately. I got too tired and went to bed that night, which is a pity because I am told he was very good. I'm told he made a hat like mine and compelled Madame to wear it. I would certainly have liked to have seen that. He certainly made a name for himself, which is a difficult thing for a ventriloquist to do because it's an act that doesn't lend itself to television. It's a live spectacle best seen in clubs or at the theater.

We also had entertainment from Rita Moreno[42], who was wonderful. Then there was a singing quartet whose stage name I can't remember. My contribution was to have tea with the guests and tell them how to be happy. On one such occasion a group of us were having tea and I had begun answering people's questions. Ms. Moreno then said, "I have a question. Is there anything you think that isn't a mistake?" And I replied loudly, "You are not a mistake!" And everybody cheered and clapped.

I did enjoy going on gay cruises, but I don't do them anymore as it's really an upheaval. We never went on the high seas, only on the middle seas. We once went to the Cayman Islands, where they tried to prevent us getting off when they realized we were a gay cruise. Then we went on to Nassau, the capital of The Bahamas. Then to Ocho Rios, which is the most depressing place ever. It's on the northern coast of Jamaica, I think, and there is no beach. Or not one that I saw, anyway. Instead, there is a flat mud space between the water and the jungle. And on that flat space there are huts with corrugated iron rooms, where people sit outside posing like a nation of Madame Butterflies. They wait for the ships, and when the ships come in they come down to the water's edge to sell you anything and everything, including themselves.

When we made landfall at Ocho Rios, I was attached to two women who were great fun. We hired a car and went

[42] Rita Moreno, Puerto Rican actress, dancer and singer

throughout the length and breadth of the land, all of which was mud or jungle and then we came back. I found out that the two women I traveled with had become rich by living in various places in Florida. They would buy a property, posh it up and resell it for a great profit. They were the Donald Trumps of Florida! It's a strange way of earning a living, but it made them rich.

One of the ladies was called Lee and each morning aboard the cruise ship, she would come into the dining room and say, "Hi, everybody."

And everybody would say, "Hi, Lee!" back. This became the ritual sound not only at breakfast but also at lunch, tea, and supper. She was a remarkable woman because she wore a different evening dress every day. She must have traveled with an entire set of suitcases.

15. HOMOSEXUALS

I remember once doing a performance of my one-man show in Boston. We had reached the question-and-answer section and a young man asked me, "Should I tell my mother I am gay?"

And I said, "Never tell your mother anything!"

Then later, just as I was leaving the theatre, I found the young man standing and waiting for me. By his side was a white-haired little old lady. He said, "When you said never tell my mother anything, she was with me."

I turned to the little old lady, but before I could say anything, she said, "I'm with you, I don't want to know."

This episode therefore reinforced my long-held opinion. They really don't want to know. What are they supposed to say? "I congratulate you," or "Don't tell your father!" or "How terrible for you," or "What?"

You see, a large number don't want to hear the words. When that woman was told her son was gay, she then knew the truth, which of course she had known in a way all the time. Previously, when the neighbors had said to her, "Your youngest son is so good-looking. Why is it I never see him with a girl?" She would reply, "I don't know. Maybe he's just not met the right girl." But now she knows the truth.

So now when the question is asked she is either forced to lie or she blushes, tears come into her eyes and she runs indoors. My advice is simple: don't tell anybody anything unless they ask. By asking they are saying they are ready for the truth to impact their lives.

The truth is that, by the time you are twenty-nine, they will know anyway. Or as good as know. They will know something's up and they will draw their own conclusions. Possibly they will talk about it amongst themselves and arrive at the right conclusion and everything will be alright.

Why gay men are still called 'gay' I can't imagine, because these days they are all so angry. And before they were angry, they were miserable. So, I think gay in the traditional meaning is the last thing that they are. There is, of course, a kind of hysterical gaiety among gay men, which was once described by Mr. Proust.[43] He said, "The laughter of homosexuals is a spasm, convulsing the knees and the wrists." It sounds catty until you realize that Proust was gay himself, so he is being equally disparaging to himself as well as to others.

I remember when the gay community decided to use the word 'queer' as an identifier and reclaimed the word from those who had turned it into a slur. Christopher Isherwood[44] and I never minded the word queer, even when it was meant to be an insult. I think we both recognized it was only a word, and there was no good getting worked up about it.

But returning to the word 'gay', I have never known any group of people less gay than the gay community. They

[43] Marcel Proust was a French novelist

[44] Christopher Isherwood, British-American novelist

are serious about everything. Everything is an affront these days. Everything is a wrong. They must be tired of marching up and down the streets. They should know that you don't gain a good public image by walking in and out of cathedrals and interrupting communion services. To me it's all a little aggressive. Too demanding.

I admit, however ,that the gay population has a problem when someone like Matthew Shepard is murdered. It is a very serious thing, if he was really only murdered because he was gay. At the trial of his murderers there were people standing outside the courtroom saying the boys had done the right thing. That homosexuality must be stamped out! And I saw those statements broadcast on television! His was such a terrible, terrible death, and a reminder to us that such violence still goes on.

I do however think it's an unalterable law that anger begets anger. I do think many actions by the gay community have backfired because, if you shake your fists in the face of society, it will do the same to you.

My personal belief is that it would have been better to have been quieter. That's taking the long-term view however, and I must say that most gay Americans do not share my patience. They want everything to be now.

I would wish it would change. I wish that homosexuals would just go on living their lives and not always be demonstrating, shouting, screaming, carrying on and disturbing everything.

You see, to real people, homosexuals these days only represent trouble. People used to say to me in England, "What do they want now?" This was because they thought gay men and women were always asking for something. Always wanting to go somewhere, be something or say something. I fear it only comes across as attention-seeking and trouble-making.

Nowadays, homosexuals look around for something that they have been denied and insist on having it. Gay men serving in the military is a case in point. When I ask them if they really want the right to be a killing machine they say, "No. No. But I would be prepared to shoot somebody if the circumstances demanded it." That's not what a soldier is like! A soldier loves to kill and they count the number of people they shoot. They say, "There they are!" Bang! Bang! Bang! "Got four of them!" And that's the way a soldier's mind has to work or else he can't be a soldier. I don't think most gay men have any idea of that.

And I have never understood why gay men want long-term relationships. To my mind, there is a weird insufficiency in being gay. Gay people feel inadequate. They want to be just as good as real people, so they want everything that real people have. Hence their desire for long-term relationships. But this is a mistake, not just for gay men, but for their heterosexual brothers and sisters. Gay people deny that they want to be normal, but it is visible for everyone to see. They want everything except their sexual preference to be just like the rest of the world.

They feel like outsiders. They say they want to be separate but equal, but I don't think they do. I once said to a gay man, "A gay person is somebody standing on the bank watching other people swim."

He responded rather defensively to me, "Oh, I'm swimming alright!" I took this to mean he was having a jolly time, rather than that he was part of the real world.

I know my opinion is a minority one within the gay community, although I have met others who share my views. I accept, however that they are old-fashioned. They represent the time in which I grew up when the world was very different.

Every minority that has fought against oppression for

acceptance or for so-called 'rights' has always had dual forces within it. Some advocate for radical change. Others for an approach that doesn't rock the boat. Some want immediate acceptance. Others plead for assimilation rather than confrontation.

As you can tell, I am more for the gradual approach. Partly this is because of my life experience. Partly this is because I am weary. I have also learned that it is better to ask for nothing. That way you are never disappointed.

I would however point out one flaw in the gay community's plan to become real people with the exception of their sexual preference, and it is this: when there is nothing to distinguish us from real people, we will have less and less in common with one another. At that point the gay community will cease to be a community at all. At that point we may end up joining the real world, but it will be at the downfall of our own.

16. TELEVISION HOSTS

I personally like television. If I have any ambition at all, it is to meet everybody in the world before I die. I'm not doing badly. You cannot listen to everyone, of course, but you can speak to them on television. It's an excellent opportunity, a wonderful medium.

More precisely, my appreciation is for that much-maligned, although much-loved, much-watched and even listened-to form of television called the talk show.

People, often in a panic, sometimes telephone me to say, "I have to go on television. Have you any advice to give me as to how I should conduct myself?" I reply, "It's like a party. Dress up and look pleased to be there." After all, the operative words are 'host' and 'guest'. But this advice must be taken calmly. There are strategies, which I won't go so far as to call secrets, to navigate the territory of television. Allow me to share them with you.

First, do not wear anything spectacular such as sequins. They will catch the light and distract attention from your face. And when I say, "look pleased," I do not mean that you should smile broadly. It will emphasize the lines on your face. Like all people who are in the public eye, you must wear an expression of fatuous affability. Turn toward the lights, but never blink. The only time you can shut your eyes is when the host is speaking. With any luck, the cameras will be turned away from you then.

Secondly, understand that the experience of doing a talk show begins long before you are on camera. Some channels lead you straight to a make-up room where an expert paints you bright orange, to counteract the bluish tint of the television lights. It's a good idea for a guest to carry a pocket mirror so you can take a crafty peek at what has been done to you in case it is absolutely terrible. And remember not to put your hands near your face because they will not have been made up to match.

Other stations lead you into a green room and from there onto the stage, so be prepared. For some unknown reason, cameramen do not like you to wear large areas of black or white. Wear smart, new, unemphatic clothes.

I could say that guests have nothing to fear, but unfortunately some interviewers try to score points off you. While the metaphor of a party may be true, to some the metaphor of a boxing match, automobile race or skeet shoot is closer.

An English interviewer, now fortunately dead, asked Mr. Tati[45] why Englishmen thought that all Frenchmen were pigs. Mr. Tati rose from his chair and left the screen. Somebody had to run after him and coax him back. Mr. Tati did the right thing. Never argue with a television host. Never defend yourself. In fact, never display any strong emotion at all. It may embarrass the viewers.

The same man was interviewing Ms. Swanson[46]. She was a woman, about 30 years older than he, a movie star

---

[45] Jacques Tati, a French comedian

[46] Gloria Swanson, American actress

and an American. That placed her just south of being a saint, but when she pronounced the word 'schedule' in American (skedule) instead of in English (shedule), he turned to the camera and made a face of disgust. Ms. Swanson ignored him. Nothing said in front of the cameras need be taken seriously.

Only one law governs television: the survival of the glibbest. If you're asked, "What is the secret of the universe?" don't gasp, don't cough and don't say, "A good question." That shows you're playing for time. Say immediately and calmly, "I'm happy to tell you there is no secret." The remark is inane but you smile and your lips move. You'll be back.

A television interview, you see, is like a geography examination. You can't study the whole world. Therefore, on the night before your exam, you take your atlas down from its shelf and open it at random. The map that you happen to expose is of China. You regard this as a sign from You-Know-Who and study China. The next day the main question in your paper is about France. You-Know-Who has sold you a pup. Don't panic. Your answer begins, "France is not like China, which is . . ."

Let me translate the situation into television terms. You arrive at the studio with a wonderful anecdote about your mother. When you get there, some fool says, "How's your father?" This give you a few seconds to reply, "My father's worn out coping with my mother who . . ." In other words, you say what you've come to say, no matter what the question.

Americans love what they call 'one-liners'. In other words, aphorisms. An aphorism is an untidy truth neatly phrased, but do not begin an interview with one. The interviewer and the audience may find it too much for them, but when they have become used to your style of conversation, finish the interview with one. It will give people something to remember you by. Begin by addressing the interviewer. End by speaking to the camera. The world must get the impression that you are its friend and have come to tell it something you feel it would like to know.

There is also the question of how much of you the camera can see. This you will have to guess. If the camera seems very near, then likely only your face will be visible. Do not make big movements. Keep your hands near your face. I have known a victim who stood up to demonstrate something he wished to explain. As he rose, he said to the cameramen, "Can they see my feet?" The technician adjusted his camera. They do not mind doing this, so long as you don't do it too often. It is your show. You must make the most of it. You have only about ten minutes in which to persuade the world to understand you and, above everything else, to like you.

Though certain famous interviewers try to score off you, most of them are working to show you off. You're talent and stardom reflects theirs, since you are their guest. The best in this respect is Mr. Cavett[47]. Whatever he is secretly thinking, he appears to be giving your every utterance his gravest interest and he gives everyone the impression that he likes them.

If you do not have the good fortune to be the guest of such a person, still accept any offers. You need all the television time you can acquire. If you are forced to appear with another guest you must acknowledge them, but do not give them an opportunity to speak. Your television time is short. It is sacred. Do not let someone steal your thunder.

---

[47] Dick Cavett is an American television personality

17. THE ALTERNATIVE CHRISTMAS MESSAGE

As you may know, the Queen of England addresses her subjects every year on the afternoon of Christmas Day in a broadcast on BBC television and radio. In her speech she reviews the year and invites viewers and listeners to be part of the history of Britain, to be proud of being British, and to journey onwards together.

Sometime in 1993, a television executive called Mr. Michael Jones came from England to America to meet with me. When we met he asked me, "Have you one final speech, one final message, to deliver to the people of Britain?"

And flippantly I said, "Yes, I have. Tell them to pack tonight and to leave for America tomorrow."

He seemed rather pleased by that. He told me that Channel 4 were contemplating an annual alternative to the Queen's Christmas Message.

"Will you make the inaugural alternative speech for us?"

And in typical fashion I said, "Ye-e-e-e-s-s-s-s."

Then, of course, I began to worry about it. Principally I was worried about whether or not I would have to memorize the speech. My worries were soon soothed. The producers told me I could either read it from a script or a teleprompter. This made me considerably happier about the whole thing.

So, without further ado, here is what I told the British that night, as broadcast on Britain's Channel 4 on Christmas Day in 1993:

As Mr. Dickens[48] would have said, 1993 has been the best of times and it has been the worst of times. A reginal theme has permeated my year. I have had, as some of you may know, the novel experience of appearing as a queen of England in a film adaptation of Mrs. Woolf's[49] novel *Orlando.* The film connects the many moments of English history with what I believe is called 'gender-bending'.

Having worn reginal gowns, I begin to understand why Queen Elizabeth I was not always in the best of moods. She was much troubled by relatives and in-laws, often Scottish, many of whom she axed from life and even more seriously from the social register.

Continuing my honest masquerade, I appear thus to address the entire British nation on Christmas day. I am, of course, in mufti[50]. But departing from tradition, I will not speak mainly of myself, Britain, or the strangely misnamed Commonwealth. Instead, I will speak of America. I do this because America is the land where I think, despite its faults, the best of you should be.

Mr. Bush, still president in early 1993, being an elder statesman wanted everything to stay the same, the same as

---

[48] Charles Dickers, British novelist

[49] Virginia Woolf, English writer

[50] Meaning plain or ordinary clothes

it had been in the Hollywood sunshine of Mr. Reagan's day. Now Mr. and Mrs. Clinton have entered the White House, and by political standards they are a young couple.

They watched many episodes of *Sesame Street* and they wish for change. For one thing, they want to transform America into a welfare state. They want everyone, however poor, however foreign, however idle, to be eligible for healthcare. The trouble with this grand notion is that it will cost money. A lot of it.

Americans believe in money. The dollar is not just a currency, it is a passion. This being so, it is difficult to find out how they lost so much of it, especially as they did not have Mr. Lamont[51] to guide them.

In the early 1960s, when the Kennedys reigned from the brittle splendor of their fireproof castle in Camelot, almost every country in the world owed money to the United States. In the thirty years since, this situation has been allowed to become reversed.

Just as the country in general is falling part, so is New York in particular. Viewed from a distance it looms up as a magnificent citadel of steel and glass. The Emerald City come to life. But when you live in it, it turns out to be a wreck. If you take a swift taxi drive down Fifth Avenue, your head hits the roof of the taxi cab several times. If Audrey Hepburn today wanted to enjoy breakfast at Tiffany's, she would not choose to arrive at that Mecca of diamonds by taxi cab.

In the early 1960s, not only all the money but also all the power in the world was in the hands of the United States. They could have bombed everybody, so that there was only America or ashes. There would have been no

[51] Norman Lamont, then the British Chancellor of the Exchequer.

more trouble, no more anti-Americanism. The bombing hasn't been done, because American politicians were afraid of what the neighbors would say. They want to rule the world and be loved. It can't be done.

What made Mrs., I beg your pardon, Lady Thatcher so great was that she didn't give a damn whether anybody loved her or not. That was how she became the greatest political star since Mr. Churchill. Like that great figure, she wept only for herself.

Now America is not in a sufficiently secure position to bomb the world, so it has decided to save it, which may prove to be just as expensive and will certainly take much longer.

Adding to the violence of life in general, women have now decided to become people. This is a change for the worse. Women were nicer than people. If our cities are to be populated entirely by people, life will become faster, louder and harsher. The loudness is already here. No one seems to mind.

The American young are violent because they have no inner life; they have no inner life because they have no thoughts; they have no thoughts because they know no words; and they know no words because they never converse. They would not be heard above the din that rocks the dim cellars where they gibber and twitch.

They have one word a year which means "I don't like this" and another which says "I do like this". One season you can be bad, another you can be neat, and yet another you can be cool. When you ask the young in what sense their little friends are cool, they say nothing. They cannot embellish their judgment.

Now, all our heroes are either sportsmen, whose profession obliges them to charge one another like buffalos until their injuries compel them to retire, or movie stars, who pretend to hit, kick or shoot one another or to blow up entire cities.

Though I regret all this, it does not in any way lessen my love for America. So far, I have only once been threatened in the streets of Manhattan, whereas in England I never felt safe for a moment. Indeed, it is my impression that everybody in the United States is a friend. In England, nobody is a friend.

I left England's lonely streets over ten years ago. Here there are no nice people from Tunbridge Wells eager to chill what is left of my marrow with iceberg stares. There are no royal appointments and disappointments. This city[52] instantly embraced me, and I it. I became a naked film critic[53] and, dream of dreams, almost, almost a celebrity.

I have also come to believe wholeheartedly in Mrs. Lazarus' verse inscribed on the base of the Statue of Liberty[54]. If ever there was a huddled mass, it has to be me. Everyone can see at a glance what a huddled mass I am. No one draws attention to the fact. Indeed, on occasion, I am permitted to appear in the guise of a VIP.

Recently I attended a secret screening of a movie called *Zelda*. After the film, the entire audience went to the Algonquin Hotel. There I managed to be photographed with Mr. Fairbanks and later with Ms. Warrick. Neither of

---

[52] New York

[53] A reference to his book *The Naked Civil Servant* and career as an artists' model. Quentin was also a film critic for *Christopher Street* and *The New York Native*

[54] Emma Lazarus' sonnet includes the lines "Give me your tired, your poor, Your huddled masses yearning to breathe free, The wretched refuse of your teeming shore. Send these, the homeless, tempest-tossed to me, I lift my lamp beside the golden door!"

these two luminaries had the faintest idea who I was, but neither refused for a moment to raise me to their rarefied level of royal visibility.

This is only one sign of American generosity. They are a truly openhanded people, free with their time, their money and their availability. My advice to the British is pack tonight, set out tomorrow like the Portuguese explorers of old for the land of the blessed. We are waiting for you.

18. APOLOGY

I'm told I have stepped into a political controversy because of comments attributed to me in a recent London news story[55], sensationally titled: 'Stately Homo backs call to abort gay babies.'

The article was inaccurate. I am eighty-eight years old and have never called for any public policy, certainly not the policy referred to in the headline. I'll say what I've said before when I have been dragged into political controversy: if I offended or caused anyone hurt, I apologize and withdraw my statement.

I often get into trouble, my friends tell me, because people today – even other gay people – don't understand how painful and miserable it was to be a homosexual in the early part of the twentieth century. And so, I've borrowed a tactic from Act Up[56]: I sometimes feel the need to shock people to make my point.

I was speaking of my own personal pain – in part

---

[55] 'Stately Homo backs call to abort gay babies' by Dominic Kennedy, *The Times*

[56] Act Up, the AIDS Coalition to Unleash Power, is an international direct action advocacy group working to impact the lives of people with AIDS

because I want people to better understand how harmful homophobia was to the homosexuals of my generation. Most people today don't know this and I don't know how to make them understand. And so sometimes I say shocking things.

I hope that my controversial statement won't trigger the very kind of witch-hunts and censorships that contributed to my lifelong pain. I don't mean to get involved in politics, but sometimes I get dragged into them, and if that is the case, again, I apologize if my old age has caused me to be inarticulate in my attempts to avoid causing pain to others.

Quentin Crisp

POETRY

19. COLLECTED POETRY

I don't remember my poems very well, but lately I have been trying to remember them. You see, through discussions with Mr. Ward I am beginning to revive them from a long ago past. I thought that maybe they could be made into a slender volume, but there are only a small number of them I can remember. So, instead, I have gathered what I can remember here for inclusion in this book. There were a lot more, but alas I can't remember them all.

THE WOUNDED[57][58]

What shall we say, who cringed and live,
To those who fought and died,
And what excuses shall we give?
Where can we hide?

If there's a heaven, there they live,
Our hell is at their side,
Whether they blame or, worse, forgive,
Where can we hide?

What shall we do that will assuage
For those who did not die, their pain,
Their blindness, lameness, and their rage
That it was vain?

There are no words that we can give
To those who fought and died,
To beg for pardon that we live,
Where can we hide?

---

[57] In 1996, James Adler's composition *Memento Mori - An AIDS Requiem* was premiered in Atlanta, Georgia, performed by Amor Artis Chorale and Orchestra, and released on CD in 2001 by Albany Records. This work, in nine movements, features traditional Latin, Hebrew, and English texts as well as contemporary poetry by Quentin Crisp, Philip Justin Smith, Denise Stokes, and Bill Weaver. The two poem's of Quentin's that were used were *The Haunted* and *The Wounded*.

[58] Originally printed in *Chiron Review*, Issue #81, Winter 2005 - Michael Hathaway, editor and publisher. Also titled: WHERE CAN WE HIDE: A lament to the Vietnam soldier.

THE HAUNTED[59]

Now I am dead, the cold square house is shut,
Where once I used to live and wonder why,
And every dark, uncurtained eye,
Though bleak before, is now a tone more bleak.

Upon the blue-green lawns the starlings strut,
Where once I stood and hoped that I might die.
They strut and lance with sudden beak
The blue-green blades that no one comes to cut.

And on the pathways, tended now no more,
The raindrops gathered on the underside
Of leafless boughs, drip as they dripped before,
And here I walk and wonder why I died.

[59] See footnote on previous page. Also titled: NOW I AM DEAD.

I WILL MAKE MUSIC[60]

I will make endless music, syncopated,
Shrill, sad music, out of English speech.
Your ears, to calumny habituated,
More euphonic phrasing might not reach.

I will make endless music, till the lonely
Limits of our torment have been told,
That all may hear and some, not only
Hearken, but be heartened and consoled.

I will make endless music. Say not
That the world's ears are waxed or numb,
Because I will not, dare not, may not,
See you suffer, and be dumb.

[60] Originally printed in *Chiron Review*, Issue #81, Winter 2005 - Michael Hathaway, editor and publisher.

MANIE D'AMOUR

He has laid her down among the snows.
They will not want her now.

She is too happy, too remote,
Too still the lips, so loved by those,
Too pale the face, too smooth the brow.
A scarlet line across her throat.
They will not want her now.

THE ISLAND[61]

I know now, O' my people, that the isle
on which I promised that you would be free
was ignorantly charted, or by guile,
upon an actually empty sea.

But sometimes, after night on starless night
and mists through which for days no day could smile,
a heart that love will not let sleep may sight,
through eyes that sleep has never loved, that isle.

Therefore, if you would glimpse that gleaming reef,
that gloom of green upon the shadeless main,
may you, as I, be driven mad with grief
or they, that drove you mad, be driven sane.

[61] Also called: ON STARLESS NIGHTS

THE RACKET[62]

If I had deigned to guzzle at the plate,
Whose contents seemed egregiously to please
A squalid world that I have come to hate,
Or tried to run its race with mudded knees
And absolutely no hope of success,
Could I at last, perhaps with greater ease,
Outstretch my feeble hand and try to bless
That world that said my love was a disease?
Would I have written nobler lines than these?

[62] Originally printed in *Chiron Review*, Issue #81, Winter 2005 - Michael Hathaway, editor and publisher.

THE FAULT

This is the language I was born to speak,
The words that I am doomed to say;
I am defenseless, I am weak,
And I am gay.

I am the harm for which you're not insured
Whatever premium you pay;
I am the ill of which you can't be cured,
And I am gay.

I am the fissure through the bone,
I am the flaw within the stone,
I am the tiny cloud across the sky
of evolution's perfect day;
I am the great mistake,
But I am here to stay.

THE EARLY LIGHT

I woke and, in the early light of day,
Beheld a word I knew I'd never own,
The crowd arrived but still I was alone,
And worse, I could not find the voice to say
The angry, believing phrase that would tell
That here was hell.

And as I wept and shrugged to express
My grief, the glory faded from the sky,
The crowd departed and the night came by,
I've found the voice that helps my deep distress,
I found the words, my mouth is open, but
My heart is shut.

MY SECRET PASSION[63][64]

I thought I'd tell the people
About my secret passion,
To clear the air,
I like to share,
Besides, it was in fashion.

So, first I told my doctor,
His words were not unkind,
He said, "I'm sure
We'll find a cure,"
And patted my behind.

And then I told my mother,
I thought she would be glad,
She cried a lot
and said, "Do not
say anything to Dad."

But still I told my father,
His lips began to foam,
He paced the floor
And cursed and swore
And said, "You can't come home."

And then I told my cronies,
Their attitude was critical,
They murmured, "Dearie,

---

[63] Originally printed in *Chiron Review*, Issue #81, Winter 2005 - Michael Hathaway, editor and publisher.

[64] Also published in *Van Gogh's Ear* Journal, VGE1, 2002, Ian Ayres, editor and publisher.

this is dreary.
Please don't get political."

And last, I told my boyfriend,
It roused his deepest fears,
Before he fled
he turned and said,
"I draw the line at queers."

DRINKING SONG

Let everyone lift his glass above
And give it a friendly clink,
We'll say we're drinking to life and love,
But really we'll drink to drink.
We'll say we're toasting our ladies fair,
Their eyes of blue and their golden hair,
When really we know they stink.
We'll drink to whisky and drink to gin,
That rot your guts and impair your skin
And color your eyeballs pink.
We'll say we're drinking to life and love,
But really we'll drink to drink.
And finally, as the night wears on,
Who cares what the neighbors think?
When shame and sherry and cheese are gone,
We'll say that we stink.,
We'll say that we drink,
We'll say that we drink
To drink.

Let everyone lift his glass above
And give it a friendly clink,
We'll say we're drinking to life and love,
But really we'll drink to drink.
We'll say we're drinking to absent friends,
To comrades meeting and journeys' ends,
Who cares if they swim or sink?
We'll say we're drinking to life and love,
But really we'll drink to drink,

We'll drink to white and to milky wine,
To every juice of the sacred vine,
Though some of it tastes like ink.
We'll say we're drinking to life and love,
But really we'll drink to drink.
We'll say that we drink
To drink.

PRECIOUS STONE[65]

Spring comes when spring comes never any more,
Over the barren ploughland of my years,
But I, who always feared the spring before,
Have found at last an ending to all fears,
When God, with knotted winds across the sky,
Scourges the white or weeping clouds of rain
Or, from the bed from which it loved to lie,
Drags by its emerald hair the sleeping grain,
Convulses in the agony of birth,
Trees that were old and only longed to die
Or with a rash of flowers infects the earth,
These things are like a rainbow in the sky,
If God ordained all this, he did ordain
That I who wanted love, should be alone,
I am some kindred miracle of pain,
I asked for bread, he gave me precious stone.

[65] Also titled: SPRING

THE MUSIC OF DELIUS

Under the transverse gloom of ruined sound,
A flute note rose and traveled on alone
Toward a sea, moon-grey and with no tide,
Girding the land this land shall someday be.

With naked feet upon the moon-grey ground,
Over recumbent columns of blurred stone,
Over my statue, lying on its side,
I followed soundlessly.

And, standing always on the moon-grey shore,
I knew the reason why I lived and died
And wept, and then not minded what I knew,
And then forgot and only watched the sea.

And no sail chipped its rim forever more
And no wind ever blew.

NEVER AND NEVER[66]

Never imagine that happiness is out there;
It is always in here,
Never try to be unlike other people;
Only strive to be more and more like yourself,
Never tell your mother anything;
Whatever you say will one day be used against you,
Never work; in fact, before you do anything
Always ask yourself one question:
Can I possibly get out of this?

[66] Originally printed in *Chiron Review*, Issue #81, Winter 2005 - Michael Hathaway, editor and publisher.

NO REGRETS

I never say no,
I can't say no,
I never say no to anything
Because I am told that, as I lie dying
On an iron bedstead in a rented room,
I shall not regret anything I did,
I shall regret what I didn't do, so I do
Anything so as to regret very little,
Like Madame Piaf,
I shall have no regrets.

DEATH MADE MAD

That's very difficult
And I don't know how to do this,
But death stands tall
Like the blades of wintry grass,
And sways with the snowflakes
While I graze the surface
With my fair feet.
When will it all end?

WILD BIRDS

Why the wild birds fly
I don't know, except that of course
We're all wild birds of a sort,
Don't you all think? Only some of us
Never get a chance to take flight.

EPITAPH[67]

O' hurt and hurtling clod of earth,
We have come back to you,
For now we know what freedom's worth,
We crawled, we stood,
We found we had the knack,
We walked, we ran, we flew,
We did these things because we could,
They were not good,
Forgive us, take us back.

[67] Sent to Robert Patrick for his birthday in 1995.

ALL THIS AND BEVIN TOO[68]

There's a place at the edge of the town
Where a Kangaroo walks with a frown
In the loneliest street
On the weariest feet
And, whenever he can, he looks down,

Though they say the street simply shone
With his smiles in the days that are gone.
He played hop-scotch, had fun
With the kids and would run
With one foot off the curb and one on.

But all that was before he had heeded
The wireless announcements that pleaded
Or read in the press
The distressed S.O.S.
Saying, 'KANGAROOS URGENTLY NEEDED.'

For, as soon as the meaning was plain
(And it was when he'd read it again),
Having hopped from his chair,
He had slid down the stair
And had boarded a Bakerloo train.

It was clear to him what he must do
He must offer himself to the Zoo.
But the moment he tried
The committee replied,
'We've already got plenty of you.

[68] First published in 1943.

'If you like, you may leave us your name
So that we can go into your claim
And then, doubtless, you'll hear
In the course of a year
An evasive reply to the same.

'And perhaps, in the interim, you
Would take home these forms to read through,
Paying special attention,
Perhaps I should mention,
To paragraph four-seven-two.'

So our hero returned to his room.
(O Bloomsbury, where is they bloom?)
And he lit in an attic
To make it dramatic
A candle to lighten the gloom

And he sat there and tried not to snivel
While wading through pages of drivel
Compiled in verbose
And ambiguous prose
By the servants that some had called civil,

For most of their questions were rude.
They asked what he weighed in the nude
And, as well as his size
And the shade of his eyes,
If he'd ever been formerly 'zooed.'

And the sky became black that was blue
Before all of his reading was through
And he still couldn't see

What the meaning would be
Of that paragraph four-seven-two.

It said, 'Kindly state how and when
In the future, the past or since then
Either you or your mother
Or father or brother
Has ever? And will they again?

So he called in the cat, who was good
At what cannot be quite understood,
And by dawn, weary-eyed,
They had somehow replied
To the question as well as they could.

About paragraph four-seven-two,
With the craftiest possible mew,
Said the cat, looking wise
And half closing his eyes,
'I should say, "Yes and No." People do.'

But day after day after day
Drifted by, either sunny or grey,
And, when finally came
A reply to his claim,
It was not what he'd hoped they would say.

Though they didn't say, 'No,' I confess,
Yet they certainly didn't say, 'Yes.'
They said, 'Not in as much,
Heretofore, such and such,
Notwithstanding' and 'nevertheless.'

And the Kangaroo thought that at least,

Since his chances were greatly increased
Of achieving his ends
By the help of his friends,
He must offer to make them a feast.

Now he hadn't the butter for toast
And not rations enough for a roast
But each guest brought some beer
And his egg for the year
And they drank to the health of their host.

They had bread, which they cut very thick,
And a cake that was hard as a brick.
It was mostly wood-pulp
But they all gave a gulp
And thirteen of them only were sick.

They had coffee but drank it, perforce,
With no milk and no sugar of course.
But the deadliest flop
Was a tiny lamb chop
Which they all of them knew to be horse.

But all that didn't get him much forwarder,
He stuck for an hour in a corridor,
Then in a room
That was cold as a tomb
And, because of the people, was horrider.

They asked him his birth-place and who
Were his parents and what did they do;
And they asked him what wage
And how tiny a cage
They could get him to take in the zoo.

And they told him his chances were small,
If indeed they existed at all,
And they yawned and enquired,
Looking angry and tired,
If he'd been to the local town hall.

After that he saw girls of fifteen
Who were gushingly willing but green
And others of fifty
Whose answers were shifty,
But no one an age in between.

And they said, without shame or remorse,
That they'd given his cage to a horse,
But that still, if he chose,
And could alter his nose,
He could put his name down for a course.

So they gave him a pen that was squiggly
And, feeling half sad and half giggly,
He managed to sign
On the dottiest line,
Though his signature went a bit wiggly.

They would train him, they said, in the art
That's performed by a horse with a cart,
And would teach him to neigh
In the very best way.
In September the classes would start.

And so, once having signed, willy-nilly,
He went, feeling wretchedly silly,
To school with a foal

Being trained as a mole
And a finch be trained as a filly.

And, after a term and a half,
With a jaguar and a giraffe,
He went in for a test
To see which was the best,
And they all of them tried not to laugh.

And the Kangaroo, out of the three,
Was successful alone in that he
Didn't swallow his bit,
And they had to admit
He was due for an equine degree.

But the final results of this test,
Which were posted to them on request,
Had got nothing to do
With a cage in the Zoo
As the cat, in his wisdom, had guessed,

For, suppressing a querulous mew,
He said, 'All our failure is due
To our answer, I fear,
Being rather too clear
About paragraph four-seven-two,

Because year after year after year
Will go by, either cloudy or clear,
Without ever a word
Being spoken or heard
That concerns your intended career.'

What the Kangaroo wondered was, 'Why?'

But he feared that to speak was to cry,
So he lolloped away.
There was nothing to say
But to bid all the neighbors good-bye.

On the monkey who'd lent him a hat
He bestowed a benevolent pat
On the top of his head,
With no word being said.
Then he went for a walk with the cat.

And to him, who was nearest his heart,
He announced he was willing to part
With his radio set,
With the bitter regret
That he'd listened to it at the start.

After which he turned homeward in tears
Where he settled his rental arrears.
Then he packed both his bags
And took down all the rags
That he'd used as a black-out for years.

'Of all joy and all happiness robbed,
We live,' the poor Kangaroo sobbed,
'(And I hope there's no harm
In misquoting a psalm)
Our life as a tale that is bobbed.'

He lives now on the edge of the town
Where at dusk he will walk with a frown
In the loneliest street
On the weariest feet
And, whenever he can, he looks down.

And he said to me, 'Though I've succeeded
In finding out how we're impeded,
It does puzzle me
That the posters I see
Still say, "KANGAROOS URGENTLY NEEDED."'

COME AND TRY TOO![69][70]

Keep up to the mark and don't get slack,
Intelligence here we ought not to lack!
Never be feeble and never be slow,
Girls and women are, that you know!
Sums and French are a bit of a fag
When you feel you'd rather be having a rag,
Of course you know this cannot be done,
Out of school is the time for fun;
Drawing's the nicest thing in the day,
Hours and hours at that I could stay!
Other lessons are not so bad;
Used up are our brains so when finished we're glad,
Still it's alright, not too much to do,
Everyone else ought to come and try too!

---

[69] Printed as D.C. Pratt, March 1920, *Kingswood House School Magazine*. Quentin was twelve years old. Taken from Andrew Barrow's book *Quentin & Philip*

[70] At Santo's Party House, in February 2009, Gordon Gano, the lead singer of the alternative rock band Violent Femmes, performed the following six Quentin Crisp poems at an event called "Quentin Crisp: The Naked Bon Vivant!": Come And Try Too, The Fault, I Will Make Music, Music of Delius, Never and Never, and No Regrets

ONE-MAN SHOW

20. AN EVENING WITH QUENTIN CRISP

New York City, 1999

Thank you and good evening. I've been forbidden from describing this occasion as a straight talk from a bent speaker. So instead we'll say it's like a sermon from a priest who is more sinful than his congregation. Or like a consultation with a doctor who is more ill than his patient. I am here to try to cure you of your freedom because I am convinced that it's an excess of freedom that has made everyone in the world so miserable.

I come from a time when there was so little liberty, if a girl wanted to wear nail varnish she had to leave home for good. And if a man wore suede shoes, there was nothing for him to do but to join the Foreign Legion. Now, you all wear, do, say whatever you like. Unlike other people of my generation, I would be happy for all the people who find themselves in these blissful circumstances, if I felt that they were happy. But wherever I look, people are not rejoicing. They are complaining.

In fact, throughout the world, protest has become a game any number can play. One weekend in London, my landlady got into the wrong march. That'll show you what's going on there. So, I must assume that what has made everybody in the world so angry is the element which has been added to their lives in recent times: their freedom.

Now, I know it's too late to ask you to abide by restrictions handed down to you by your pastors and your masters, your elders and your betters. So, what I think we need are chains of our own making. However heavy these may be, they will never feel as irksome as restraints placed by others. And not any old chains. We will have to have a system, and that begins with each of us trying to decide what it is that makes him the way he is. And then agreeing not to do, wear or say anything that doesn't reinforce this image.

This involves a journey to the interior. Not altogether a pleasant experience. Why? Well, because as well as totaling what you consider to be your assets, you will also have to take a long hard look at those things that your friends call, "the trouble with you." For the whole purpose of life is to try to reconcile the glowing opinion we have of ourselves with the terrible things other people say about us. The synthesis between these two opposing opinions will be your identity.

But that's not quite enough. Your identity is like your fingerprints. These too are your very own, but if they are discovered they may be used against you. Therefore, you will have to polish up your new identity until it becomes a style. Something interesting by which you are prepared, by which you are proud to be identified, and something with which you can barter with the outer world to get from it what you want. I won't say what you deserve, because if we all got what we deserved, we would starve. This polishing-up process will make your days so formal that, compared with them, the life of a Trappist monk would seem like an orgy.

Now, I know I'm rattling on about problems which by world standards would be trivial. This I understand. But I do so because never a day goes by…well, never a month goes by…without someone coming to me and saying, "Oh, you do have a nice life." Me! A nice life? This would be a reasonable remark if I lived as you do in mansions riddled with standard of living. But I don't. I live on the Lower East Side of Manhattan, just beyond redemption, in a small room which has never been cleaned in fifteen years.

Which brings me to my first message of hope: never sweep the place where you live, because after the first four years the dirt doesn't get any worse! It's just a question of not losing your nerve. I'm sure I'm right about this. The other day a woman said to me, "No wonder you're so nice to everybody, you never do any housework." So, now it transpires that all the middle- and upper-class housewives in the world are in a blind rage by half-past ten in the morning, worn out, I shouldn't wonder, with all that sweeping, dusting, and washing the dishes.

Now there's no need to wash the dishes unless you find that you've passed the fish barrier. It works like this. When you're hungry and you look at your plate and it says "bacon," you think I could eat an egg. And the next day, when your plate says "egg," you think I could eat a fish. But when you look at your plate and it says "fish", it's time to wash the dishes.

I'm only telling you these things by the way, so as to set you free from your boring domestic rituals. I want to give you some time each day when you can stop looking outward and start looking inward. Then you can decide who you truly are.

Now the next thing that my visitors say is, "Oh, you do know such wonderful people." And I do. But this too would only be a logical comment if my room was stuffed with people of wealth, influence and status. And it isn't. It's full with the denizens of the Lower East Side. And that brings me to my second message of hope: never try to keep up with the Joneses. Drag them down to your level. It's cheaper!

Then I'm asked where do I meet these wonderful people. And I say, "As a rule, in lay-about cafes." Those marvelous places where you can sit through lunch, tea and supper with one cup of coffee. I used to offer to take my friends to one of these places, but they would always mutter something like, "Of course, when we get there, you'll have to tell me what to say."

I hope I am painting for you a thoroughly depressing picture of someone who has reduced himself to the level where he envies me, and who seems to be living like a kidnapped victim in unwanted isolation only a few yards from where the traffic of the world is going by, with nothing more substantial boarding up the windows than self-doubt. The words "you'd have to tell me what to say" are a clue. They show us that we are not dealing with a dreary old search for true love. The person who wants to make friends doesn't have to think what to say, he has to learn how to listen. Now, we'd all like to have friends, but if it means you've got to listen to them, the price is ridiculous.

So what does he want? As I see it, he longs for somewhere to go and, when he gets there, for somebody to be. But where and who? When modern man looks around in search of a destiny nothing presents itself to him, as it did when I was young, as being suited to his age, his sex, his nationality, his class, and his station in life. Nowadays, whichever direction he looks in, he finds himself in a landscape without signposts, without milestones, without roads. The sheer vastness of the terrain that lies before him may make him feel small.

Now, if we are going to develop our own style, we must banish forever all thoughts that are self-diminishing. We mustn't imagine that anything we discover, when we make our journey to the interior, is too trivial or even too distasteful to present to the world. The curiosity of your neighbors is a tribute to your individuality and you should encourage it.

Never defend yourself. I am appalled by the lust for evasion, which seems to be absolutely everywhere. Even among actors, who presumably are a nation of exhibitionists. Elizabeth Taylor and Richard Burton were so great that they brought style to marriage. A difficult thing to do. And then, they brought style to divorce. But even they express the fear that the paparazzi in Rome might take pictures of them in the lavatory. Now the way to deal with that problem, if you think it is one, is not to build a higher and higher wall around your villa, but to learn to urinate with style.

All concealment is wrong. If there were none, half of the world's problems would disappear overnight. There would be no snooping, no fixing, no blackmail, and no fear in the world other than physical fear. That wouldn't be a bad start. And not only is all secrecy a sin, but it doesn't work.

My spies tell me that there are already machines which exist that can collect and tabulate all the details of everyone's private lives and store it in a space that big. Now if this can be done, it will be done, because machines are greater than men and their watchfulness is tireless and invincible. And if this is so, our attitude toward them should be existential.

Do you understand that word? An existentialist is

somebody who realizes that he can only exercise his free will by swimming with the tide but faster. Therefore, if the machines will triumph in the end, why don't we make ourselves over to them from the very beginning?

George Orwell, who wrote the book *1984*, envisioned a situation in which every private room in every house would have riveted into the wall a one-way television screen, through which you will see nothing - which might be a relief - but you would be watched by Big Brother. Orwell became completely neurotic about this, but why?

I don't know how things are here, but in London we waltz around the city with half our hair painted pink and the other half painted green, jingling with amulets, razor blades and safety pins, creating no sensation whatsoever. And when we get home we feel thoroughly defeated. But when the George Orwell setup occurs, when you get back to your room and you start to dismantle yourself, you will realize you are still of abiding interest to someone.

All you have to do to get this situation on your own terms is to decide what image of yourself you are going to present to the powers-that-be. No excuses are acceptable. I say this because whenever I suggest to anyone that he should develop his own style, he immediately says, "I am not wise enough, witty enough or handsome enough."

Beauty is a complete waste of time. Because even now, without knowing it, we still cringe in the shadow of classical ideals of beauty. The Greeks were mad about the human body, so much so that during its heyday Athens must have looked like an outfitters' window during a weavers' strike. But it didn't help. Not one of the great classical statues has the least physical individuality, which would make it interesting or desirable. So, beauty, you will never need. And I can give you further proof.

There was once a man whose name was Mr. Tillet[71], but he was known as 'The Angel'. He was shorter than I am, but he was twice as wide, and his head was as long from his chin to his crown as the skull of a donkey. His pate was bald, but the rest of his body was covered with fur, right down to his fingernails. When a prospective employer first saw him, she fainted. Nevertheless, he made more money as a wrestler in four short years than the divine Joe Louis made out of a lifetime in the boxing ring.

Now to me, Mr. Tillet's life was a positive parable of style. He took that which made him so like himself, regardless of whether it made him better or worse than other people in their eyes, and he put it in its appropriate setting. He put it where it would do the most good. And that, to my mind, is what all of you have to learn to do.

I've been forbidden to rattle on about the amount of money that Mr. Tillet made. I've been told that I equate wealth with style. I don't, but I would say this: to a physicist money would be the solid state of style. There's no other connection between the two. And of this, also, I can give you proof.

Until recently, there was in Soho - the hooligan district of London - a woman known as The Countess. But in spite of her imperial style, she had in fact no fixed address, no means of support, and her body was perpetually bent double from a lifelong habit of looking through trash cans to see whether she could find something she could sell to a kind friend or, if not, that she herself could use.

One day, in a trashcan in the most expensive part of London, she found a complete backless bead dress. She longed for night to fall, so that she could nip into a dark

[71] Maurice Tillet was a French professional wrestler

doorway and try it on. But by about half-past six, her patience had worn out. It was barely twilight, so she went into a churchyard in the middle of London and there she proceeded to take off her clothes. This attracted a crowd, which in turn attracted a policemen. And the next day in court, when the magistrate said, "And what exactly were you doing, stripping among the dead?" She replied, "I was doing what any woman would be doing at that hour. I was changing for dinner."

So you see, however grandiose the style you may choose for yourself, you will not need any actual money to support it. And more than that, you won't even need talent.

Now, I never saw Sarah Bernhardt on the stage, but I have seen a strip from a movie, showing her coming into the home stretch in *Camille*. The death scene. On a rather tacky Empire couch sits Armand, and he supports Ms. Bernhardt in a very defensive sort of way, as though she was some kind of a firecracker. Which in a way she was. And she lies opposite him wearing a minimum-risk nightdress, and she has on clown's makeup, and her hair is right down into her eyes.

Now someone must have told her it was a silent movie, but did she care? No. The moment the cameras began to run, her black lips started to move faster than those of a policeman giving corrupt evidence. And when her lips moved, her eyes began to roll. And when her eyes moved, her hand shot out into the air returning later to give her a terrible blow to the chest. Sometimes it was one arm, sometimes it was the other arm, and sometimes it was both arms together. And then as abruptly as all this activity had begun, it stopped. Her arm swung down in front of the couch, like the limb of a rag doll.

Now I am not trying to foist upon you my own philistine reactions. This movie was shown at the National

Film Theatre in London, and that is a building so highbrow that no one can obtain admission to it unless he can prove that he comes from one of the cheese-and-wine belts of England. But it made no difference. The audience choked with derisive mirth. A man near me fell out into the gangway, his feet twiddled in the air. La Divine, indeed.

It wasn't her acting that made Ms. Bernhardt divine, it was her nerve. Oh, and it was the coffin that she slept in at night, and it was the cheetah that dragged her on a gold chain through the rooms of her house. Not that I am suggesting that any of you should keep a pet. We've got enough dumb friends without them. I'm merely explaining that you won't need any talent in order to be able to project your chosen style. And nowadays, you don't even need virtue.

You no longer have to be an object of public veneration or even affection. You can be the focus of contempt, or downright hatred. After all, as a test of whether you still mean something to somebody, being loved can never be a patch on being murdered. That's when someone really has risked his life for you. And if you've decided on depravity as the fluid in which you will suspend your monstrous ego, then you will have the most wonderful examples before you. Or rather behind you, because nearly all of them are in history.

In medieval France, living at the same time as Joan of Arc, there was a great French nobleman called Gilles de Rais, and he murdered 150 choirboys in a lifetime. Now quantity is not style. All the same, it's difficult not to be impressed, isn't it?

When he was caught, de Rais did something which I wouldn't advise any of you to attempt if you're just beginners. He reversed his style. Now before you can do this, you must be absolutely sure that the image that you're taking up is more blinding than the one that you've abandoned.

On the first day of his trial, de Rais was his usual dreary imperious self, refusing to take any notice of what his accusers told him on the grounds that they were not his social equals. On the second day, he repented. He confessed so long, so loud and so much, that the bishop who was trying his case rose and covered with a cloth the face of the crucifix hanging on the courtroom wall. Now I dwell on this dramatic gesture only to show you that style begets style. That means that when you've completed your image of yourself, you won't be surrounded by born-receivers of the news. Your style will magnetize toward you other stylists, and you will be able to enjoy them and yourself.

Finally, when he was condemned to death, de Rais cried out, "I am redeemable!" And this brought people from far and wide throughout France to pray for his soul. And some of those people were the parents of the children he had murdered. If this is not style, it is at least gesture on a national scale, all brought about by one great man.

Of course, before you can build some such dizzying, dazzling structure as a monument to yourself, you must first get the foundations of your private life absolutely solid. From now on, I think you should try to regard your home as your dressing room and the world as your stage. And at home, there must be nothing which doesn't represent the kind of person you have decided to become. It doesn't matter if your home is full of gadgets which are advertised on television every twenty minutes. They've got to go!

And when you've gotten rid of the superfluous things, you start on the unnecessary actions. From now on, there should be no doodling, and no hobbies, and I used to say there must be no daydreaming. But now I have changed my opinion, and I think you are allowed your daydreams up to the age of twenty-five, but after that they may become an alibi. You understand me? It's no good running a pig farm badly for thirty years, while saying "really I was meant to be a ballet dancer." By that time, pigs will be your style.

And it follows logically. If there is to be no doodling and no hobbies, there ought to be no evening classes. Do you have evening classes here? Well, it is alright if you're going to learn to sing and dance, because these are activities the results of which you take out into the world and wear like a crown. People who've learned to sing will always have richer, rounder voices. People who've learned to dance will always have bigger, bolder movements. But as for pottery and basket-weaving, what good are they? The moment the doors of the evening institute clang shut behind you, you're back where you started. On the way home, you might get into an argument with a stranger at a bus stop and be left saying, "Well, I can't express myself. You'll have to come and see one of my baskets."

And once you've rid yourself of the unnecessary actions, you'll next need to focus on the superfluous people in your life. I've been forbidden to say that each of you must live alone. I've been told my attitude toward cohabitation is glib. So I will lean toward true love and say that if you are actually stuck with somebody, you had better stagger on with them. It's the very best I can do.

Until recently, I had no opinions about cohabitation. But in the last two years, I've become a kind of mail-order guru. People write to me, and then they come and see me. Most of the people who do this are very young and I know why they visit me. It's in order to get the edge on their parents.

Recently a girl of fifteen turned up and she got me to

write my name on a piece of paper, and the moment I stopped, she said, "I can't make up my mind whether to show this to my mother or not." She was going to save it for her darkest hour. When her mother says, "You dress yourself like a harlot. You do nothing that your father wishes. You use this house as a hotel." She's going to say, "You don't know the half of it, mother. I've met Quentin Crisp!"

And the other people who come to see me are women in middle life. Over and over again, they ask me the same burning question: "Is there life after marriage?" The answer is, "No." The constant proximity of another person will cramp your style, fatally in the end, unless that person is somebody you love and then the burden will become unbearable at once.

How can anybody begin each dawn with a fresh assault upon his style, if the moment he opens his eyes, he hears a voice beside him say, "And another thing. . .?"

And if going around in pairs is bad, it's even worse going around in a heap. Never be seen tagging along at the tail end of a demonstration. Never be found hopping up and down on the fringe of a pop group. And above all, never, never strike. Do you have strikes here? When I talk to men about strike action, they always say, "It's alright for you. You don't have a wife and kids." I can tell from the sound of their voices that men regard a family as suffering incurred in a moment of weakness. Even so, you must never strike. There is danger in numbers. They may nudge you into performing an action which is beyond the limits of your chosen style, and in public.

The striker makes demands on the dreary grounds that he is one of many, all of whom are alike. But the stylist asks for what he wants in the name of the fact that he is unique. And everything in the world, except diamonds, is subject to the law of scarcity value. When the time for serious bargaining comes, you will win.

But, of course, it is not enough merely to get the foundations of your home life squared up. You also have to decide what you are going to do in the outer world. Some of you may be so old-fashioned that you still have jobs. If this is so, try not to get stuck in work where you deal only with things. And I include the highest possible level of things: sculpture, books and paintings. They are only objects, just like washing machines, but not as useful.

It would be difficult for me to translate the dilemma that lies before the visual artist into American terms. But in England, if I could show you a huge great piece of concrete with a hole in it, everyone would say, "It's a Henry Moore." But if I could drag on Henry Moore himself, nobody would know who he was. So all that chipping, all that chiseling, it's been in vain. You must have a job where you deal with people, because then every waking working hour you will be secretly polishing up your techniques of self-projection.

There are plenty of such jobs available. There's preaching. All the great evangelists in the world have been American, so this shouldn't be difficult for you. Before any of you were born, I saw Amy Semple MacPherson. Magnificent, dressed in white from head to foot, with scarlet hair up to here, and she said, "The Lord has sent out his angels on speed bikes of mercy." You can try something like that.

If you don't want to be a preacher, you can be a teacher. Teaching is also very stylish, because the material with which you are working is nearly always children and teenagers, and they have built-in publicity value. It doesn't matter if you encourage them or repress them, you're in!

The great teaching stylist was a man called Mr.

Braithwaite[72]. He wrote a book called *To Sir, With Love.* It caused a great sensation when it was first published, but in that book there is not one sentence about education, about whether history is easier to teach than geography. It is full of what the children, their parents, and the other members of the staff thought about the writer. So, now we know that whatever anyone says he was teaching, his subject was always himself. Teaching is for teachers, and not for students. And this principal pervades throughout the professions. The stage is for actors, not for audiences. Religion is for priests, not for congregations. Politics are for politicians, not for voters.

If you can't be a teacher, if there's nothing that you know and they don't, then you can try politics. The great political stylist was Mrs. Peron[73]. I don't know whether any of you realize in what a personal and, at the same time, pervasive way she ruled her kingdom.

In England, spelling primers begin with the words "the cat sat on the mat." No wonder literacy is at a low ebb, when the first glimpse of it is this banal and even distasteful piece of information. But in Argentina, spelling books began, "I love Evita." And the crowning moment of her entire career was when she stood on the balcony of the Casa Rosada, in Buenos Aires, to make a speech. She lifted her hands to the crowd. And as she did so, with a sound like railway trucks in a siding, the diamond bracelets slid from her wrists. When the expensive clatter had died away, her speech began "Guerra: Nosotros, los descamisados…" We are the shirtless ones!

---

[72] E. R. Braithwaite was a Guyanese-born, British-American novelist

[73] María Eva Duarte de Perón was the wife of Argentine President Juan Perón and First Lady of Argentina

Now, I don't really believe in Mrs. Peron, but the Argentineans did and still do. So much so, that when she died, they petitioned the pope to make her a saint. His holiness declined. But if he had consented, what a triumph for style that would have been! A double-fox stole, ankle strap shoes and eternal life. Nobody's ever had that.

But if you feel preaching or teaching are insufficiently physical to embody your idea of yourself, then there's sport. Did you know that Mohammed Ali said, "The boxing was only to bring me to the people." Think of that. All that diet, all that abstinence, all that downright suffering. They were only to raise him to a level from which he could still further extend his image. And if you think he hasn't done so, remember this: the fight before 'the final triumph' was never once referred to as the contest that that unknown gentleman won. It was always regarded as the fight that Muhammad Ali lost. So, now we realize that having a lifestyle doesn't even depend on winning or doing things right.

But if you feel that you'll never get up early enough in the morning even to be an indifferent sportsman, all is still not lost. Because the career that will give you the most direct route to self-fulfillment is the stage. And nowadays, you don't even have to go on the stage, because all professions whatsoever are also the career of acting. This is because television has become inextricably woven into our lives. No politician can hope to win votes unless he looks good on television. We have Sunday programs that make you feel that no bishop is ever going to bless any part of the congregation which doesn't happen to be kneeling under the arc lights. And we have medical programs that make you feel that no surgeon is going to bother to cut out of your middle anything that he doesn't think worth showing to the television cameras.

It stands to reason that if you want to propagate your image, you'll have to go into television. And you'll have to stay there. As Mr. Coward[74] said, "Television is not for watching, it's for being on." And it's easier to do than you imagine, because only one law prevails on television: the survival of the glibbest.

If, for instance, a televisionary asks you, "What is the secret of the universe?" It is no good stammering and saying, "A..a…a good question." You're finished. What you do when the televisionary asks you "What is the secret of the universe?" You say, "I am happy to tell you all that there is no secret." The remark is inane, but you're smiling and your lips are moving. You'll be back.

A television interview is like a geography exam. You can't study the whole world. So, the night before the exam, you take your atlas from its shelf and you open it. It says, "China." So, you study China. And the next day, in the exam, you discover the main question in your paper is, "France." So your answer begins, "France is not like China, which. . . ."

I'll translate that, if I can, into television terms. If you arrive at the studio with a wonderful antidote about your mother, and some clot says, "How's your father?" You've got a few seconds in which to say, "Thank you, my father's worn out coping with my mother, who. . . ." In other words, you say what you've come to say no matter what the question.

You must also remember, when you think about the stage, that the journey made by an actress from anonymity to stardom is the path that all of you must tread in one context or another. At the beginning of her career, an

---

[74] Noël Coward was an English playwright, composer, director, actor and singer

actress plays a great number of very different parts, anything she can get actually. And at that stage, she says that what she enjoys is the variety. Later on, it's noticeable that she plays fewer, more closely related parts. In the second half of her career, an actress says that what she likes is the opportunity to study character in depth. She means her own, because finally, with luck, she finds the one part which fits in every detail her dream of herself.

I'm so old that I knew Bette Davis when she was a nice girl. But after many long dark years, she was finally given the part of Regina in *The Little Foxes* and this gave her the chance to say, "Very well then, die!" And what do we learn from the glaring eyes and the mouth worn upside down? These features tell us that those were the words she'd been waiting to say since 1936.

Now, once an actress has found her ideal part, from that moment onward she never looks forward. She has given up the profession of acting and has entered the profession of being. And this, as I see it, is where all of you in the end belong.

Are you still with me? Do you understand this idea? Good, because there is a very special glow which surrounds people who have succeeded in synthesizing their professional and their personal lives.

Joan Crawford appeared in any number of movies in which she rose from rags to a position of worldly power. And in real life she finally married Mr. Pepsi-Cola. And she had all the luck in the world, because he died. This meant that she herself could enter the boardroom of that vast empire, where presumably she said, "Who told you to read the minutes?" Just like she did in all of her movies.

I saw Joan Crawford at the National Film Theatre. A car as long as the Thames drew up, and from it stepped those two now-famous children. They stood in the lobby looking bewildered. And no wonder, for after about three minutes, Ms. Crawford came out of the same car and kissed the children as though she hadn't seen them for months.

I had gone up a few steps in order to have a really good view, and for a second she saw me with those great alligator eyes. It felt as though my silhouette were being burned onto the wall behind me. She was radioactive with belief in herself. And not only will having a lifestyle bestow upon you this massive self-confidence, but it will improve the texture of the entire world through which you move.

I am told that we live in a sex-ridden society. Personally I would say that we live in a world corroded with envy. This I have no difficulty in substantiating. When I turn on my television, what does it show me? Someone stomping through streets, screeching for equal pay, equal opportunity. Equal is a dead word. Never take as your goal in life the desire to be anybody's equal. Once you have entered the profession of being, you have become a professor of a subject on which you are the only living authority. What other people do with their life, with their style, will not matter. In fact, every morning you should say to yourself, and preferably aloud, "Other people are a mistake."

No. I withdraw that remark. It might be thought sweeping. Say instead to yourself, "Concern with other people is a mistake." Now I know that this is not what most people teach you, but I am trying to spare you that traditional scramble for mutual self-sacrifice. Altruism is a debilitating, fragmenting process. But the constant watch over and the perfection of your idea of yourself, and the presentation of it gift-wrapped to others, that is a unifying and invigorating way of life, both for you and those you meet. And it carries with it a built-in invitation to the party at the end of the world, that glittering function at which everybody will be speaking and nobody will be listening.

And if you are armed with your style, you will be able to run toward that happy hubbub without the faintest fear that you may be out of your depth. Without the faintest doubt but that you will shine. And more important than either of these, the burdens of your sorrowful and angry freedom will fall away from you. You will know who you are, you will know where you are going.

Andy Warhol is said to be famous chiefly for being famous, and that suggests that he would have something to say about lifestyle and he did. He promised to each of us a quarter of an hour of fame before we die. All I am trying to do here, this evening, is to place into the hands of anybody who wishes to receive it the philosophy and the techniques by means of which he will be able to augment that mere moment of glory, so that it becomes a whole long wonderful lifetime.

Now, I see that I have rattled on too long. What we usually do now is have a pause and a good cry. In your programs you will see bits of paper on which you can write questions. This is for those who do not wish to be identified. If you don't fear identification, you will speak to me from where you sit. I only want to be sure that I say the words you wish to hear.

Thank you.

21. A CONVERSATION WITH YOU-KNOW-WHO

Taken from a personal letter written to Ian Ayres.

[Tap Tap]

YKW: Come in.

[Silence]

YKW: Well?

Me: I've arrived.

YKW: So what?

Me: I thought I had to announce my arrival.

YKW: Whatever for?

Me: I don't know. I'm sorry. Shall I go?

YKW: By all means.

Me: Where shall I start?

YKW: Anywhere. You're not going to like it here, you know.

Me: I thought I was in Heaven.

YKW: It's a Hell of a place. You'll have to learn to play the harp, for one thing.

Me: Oh, g—. I mean, dear me!

YKW: I never liked you.

Me: Nor I you, Sir.

YKW: Good. Now we've got that straight.

Me: Goodbye, Sir.

YKW: Goodbye. I don't expect we'll see each other again.

[Silence]

QUENTIN CRISP
A BIBLIOGRAPHY

In Chronological Order

1. *Lettering for Brush and Pen* (1936), Quentin Crisp and A.F. Stuart, Frederick Warne Ltd. Manual on typefaces for advertising.

2. *Colour In Display* (1938), Quentin Crisp, also illustrated by Quentin Crisp. The Blandford Press. Manual on the use of color in window displays.

3. *All This and Bevin Too* (1943), Quentin Crisp, illustrated by Mervyn Peake, Mervyn Peake Society. Parable, in verse, about an unemployed kangaroo.

4. *The Naked Civil Servant* (1968), Quentin Crisp, Jonathan Cape. Crisp's account of the first half of his life.

5. *How to Have a Life Style* (1975), Quentin Crisp, Cecil Woolf. Essays on charisma and personality.

6. *Love Made Easy* (1977), Quentin Crisp, Duckworth. Fantastical, semi-autobiographical novel.

7. *Chog: A Gothic Fable* (1979), Quentin Crisp, Methuen. Illustrated by Jo Lynch, Magnum (1981).

8. *How to Become a Virgin* (1981), Quentin Crisp, Duckworth. Second instalment of autobiography, describing his experience of the fame that *The Naked Civil Servant* and its dramatization brought.

9. *Doing It With Style* (1981), Quentin Crisp, with Donald Carroll, illustrated by Jonathan Hills, Methuen. A guide to thoughtful and stylish living.

10. *The Wit and Wisdom of Quentin Crisp* (1984), Quentin Crisp, edited by Guy Kettelhack, Harper & Row. Compilation of Crisp's essays and quotations.

11. *Manners from Heaven: a divine guide to good behaviour* (1984), Quentin Crisp, with John Hofsess, Hutchinson. Instructions for compassionate living.

12. *How to Go to the Movies* (1988), Quentin Crisp, St. Martin's Press. Movie reviews and essays on film.

13. *Quentin Crisp's Book of Quotations*, also published as *The Gay and Lesbian Quotation Book: a literary companion* (1989), edited by Quentin Crisp, Hale. Anthology of gay-related quotes.

14. *Resident Alien: The New York Diaries* (1996), Quentin Crisp, Alyson Publications. Diaries and recollections from 1990–94.

15. *The Last Word* (2017), Quentin Crisp, edited by Phillip

Ward and Laurence Watts, MB Books. The third and last installment of Quentin Crisp's autobiography, written during the last two years of his life.

16. *And One More Thing* (2018), Quentin Crisp, edited by Phillip Ward and Laurence Watts, MB Books. Quentin's last book. A compilation of essays on other people, includes his collected poetry and script for his one-man show.

ABOUT THE AUTHOR

Quentin Crisp (Dec 25, 1908 - Nov 21, 1999) was an English-born writer, actor, eccentric and raconteur. He became famous from the publication of his 1968 autobiography *The Naked Civil Servant*, which chronicled the oppression he faced as a homosexual in England before, during and after World War II, when being gay was illegal, as well as his careers as a book designer, prostitute and artist's model. *The Naked Civil Servant* later became an award-winning film starring John Hurt. Crisp performed a one-man show, *An Evening With Quentin Crisp*, which he toured nationally and internationally and which won an L.A. Drama Critic's Circle award. Crisp moved to New York at the age of 72, where he wrote books on style, culture and manners, appeared in numerous films and published a second autobiography, *How To Become A Virgin.* He was the inspiration for Sting's hit song *An Englishman In New York*. The third and final installment of his autobiography, *The Last Word*, was published posthumously in 2017, while *And One More Thing*, his last book, was published in 2018 and includes his collected poetry and the script of his one-man show.

Printed in Dunstable, United Kingdom

66602717R10111